# BDSM Relationships

# Pitfalls and Obstacles

# BDSM Relationships

# Pitfalls and Obstacles

Peter Masters

Books in the present series:

*Understanding BDSM Relationships*

*BDSM Relationships - How They Work*

*BDSM Relationships - Pitfalls and Obstacles*



Also by Peter Masters:

*The Control Book*

*Look Into My Eyes - How To Use Hypnosis To
Bring Out The Best In Your Sex Life*

*This Curious Human Phenomenon - An
exploration of some uncommonly explored aspects
of BDSM*

Cover art by Peter Masters

http://www.peter-masters.com/

ISBN 978-1-4774-6775-6

# Contents

# Chapter 1

# Introduction

Having a successful BDSM relationship isn't just about the times when things go right. Just as in any relationship, there are times when things don't go right. The range of challenges which can confront you as you wrangle your relationship from one critical point to the next is extensive. These can be the same sorts of issues which beset any relationship such as communications breakdowns or external stress. Or they can be problems and challenges which are unique to BDSM, or they can simply be vanilla issues with a BDSM twist.

One difficulty in all of this is that in BDSM we often don't have any role models. Our wider society perhaps tolerates BDSM, but it certainly doesn't promote it. In movies, on TV, and in the press we might get to see both the light and dark sides of vanilla relationships, but the weekly TV dramas with perennially happy endings and the midday chat shows with dysfunctional couples don't give us BDSM folk any hints at all. We simply don't see any constructive attempts to portray BDSM. Chick flicks don't deal with romance in rope, home-renovation reality shows never include dungeon makeovers, men's magazines don't show you how to turbo-charge your BDSM toy-bag, and dating advice columns don't talk about the best places to go to pick up a partner who likes pain play.

A consequence of this is that we can first enter into BDSM more ignorant than a pimply-faced youth on their first date. What happens on a first BDSM date? Do you kiss? What is the BDSM equivalent of foreplay? Who provides the rope? What do you say?

In earlier books of this series, I explored the nature of BDSM itself, why we do BDSM, and what we get out of having a BDSM-rich relationship with a partner. I also looked at what goes into a BDSM relationship and at what gives it its shape. In this book, I want to begin looking at what can go awry when you are trying to establish or maintain a BDSM relationship with someone.

Because of the lack of role models, many people try to press-gang vanilla role models into BDSM service. This is often like fitting a round peg into a square hole and is, at best, a poor fit. Because there often aren't friends, family, people in the local community, movie characters, TV stars, talk-show hosts, or newspaper columnists who live the dream and show us what BDSM can be like, many people try to take something or someone they do know from their vanilla experience, dress them up in BDSM leathers, and then use them as their model.

The problem with this is that the same expectations which we might have in a vanilla relationships can very rarely be applied to a BDSM relationship. That's not to say that we shouldn't find our BDSM relationships as happy and rewarding as any vanilla relationship might be, but the road to getting there is often entirely different. If you try to use the same road—the same behaviours and attitudes—in a BDSM relationship as you do in a vanilla one, then you risk creating just a vanilla relationship in BDSM clothing, and that's not likely to do anyone much good.

In book one I listed three characteristics, or pillars, which define BDSM and BDSM relationships. In short they are:

1. Disparity or unequalness of power. This is where what we do with our partner is driven in its effectiveness by one of us being in a stronger or more motivated position than the other,

2. Penetration. This is not sexual penetration, but instead is designing what we do so that it deeply affects our partner, regardless of whether sex is involved or not, and

3. Engagement. This is where what we do to and with our partner is based on what we know about them intimately and personally so that our actions are targeted at them specifically. This is as opposed to just doing things which most people like hoping that our partner will like them also.

Pitfalls and obstacles to BDSM relationships have to do with one or more of these three things breaking down. While such a breakdown doesn't necessarily mean that the two people in the relationship go their separate ways, it does mean that the nature of the relationship changes. Instead of being a BDSM relationship, it might become a vanilla relationship. Of course, if BDSM was the main "glue" holding the two people together in the first place, it may mean that they actually do go their separate ways.

Because BDSM relationships are about disparity of power, penetration, and engagement, this book is about what can prevent these pillars developing, or what can cause them to crumble.

Communication, of course, will be a major factor, as will trust. I'll get to these in upcoming chapters. Ignorance and fear can also play a surprisingly important role in BDSM relationships falling over. The intensity of feelings which BDSM can engender can be quite scary. It can be easy to unconsciously avoid this fear by enacting certain behaviours which limit engagement and penetration. Later I'll be looking at examples of both common and unconscious behaviours which do precisely that.

For now, and before moving on to the next chapter, I'd like to ask you to reflect on the nature of your own BDSM relationships and experiences.

1. Is what you do with your partner deeply and profoundly satisfying?

2. Do you feel completely satisfied at the end of the scenes you do together?

3. Do your scenes end with you feeling as if something were missing, but you don't know what?

4. In your wider relationship, is your partner doing what seem to be all the right things and yet you don't feel that all your needs are being met?

# Chapter 2

# The False Self

I'd like to now tie one of the three characteristics of a BDSM relationship, engagement (which I mentioned in the last chapter), to something I wrote about in an earlier book, namely the False Self[1].

The False Self is a persona which we create and which we present to the world to help us be accepted. For example, you may really enjoy BDSM, find it deeply satisfying, and outside of the office it may be one of the most important things you do, but at work or in the office this side of you stays hidden. How you behave at the office is conventional and conservative. Often it needs to be this way because showing up in your best leathers may not be the right way to get a promotion or keep your job. This persona you present at the office is not your real self. Or,

---

[1][MASTERS2008, pp. 93 - 96]

at most, it's just a subset of your real self with many bits hidden away.

A consequence of this is that you generally can't get your BDSM wants and needs met at the office in the same way you can when you are in your leathers or when you're tied up and being flogged. Because the real you can't be there in all your BDSM glory at the office, your real BDSM needs can't be met there. In terms of BDSM wants and needs this is, of course, unsatisfying, and this same sort of unsatisfying situation exists any time the BDSM part of us must be hidden away, such as when we're with vanilla friends, with family, with other parents we meet at preschool, in parliament, and so on.

Just because your BDSM side is not on display doesn't mean it's not there, and it doesn't mean that it's not there in other people as well. But because where you are compels you to suppress or hide your BDSM interests, it means that those around you can't engage that aspect of you, even if they were similarly inclined. The self you present in these circumstances isn't the real you. It is a false you which you display to suit the situation and to lubricate your interactions with people. When wearing your leathers or wearing nothing more than a rope harness might introduce friction with those around you, a more socially acceptable (and partly false) image can remove that friction.

Compare this to a situation where, for example, two friends— one dominant, the other submissive—are out somewhere together. Even if they don't have an intimate relationship or don't usually play together, they can still recognise their BDSM natures and engage each other in ways that are much more satisfying than if they were compelled to wear vanilla personas.

Sometimes society, ego, and other pressures can push us to create a persona which isn't just a subset of our real self, but is instead part us and part invention. Young vanilla guys, for example, might puff themselves up physically or tell exaggerated stories about their adventures to attract the ladies. The same thing can happen to someone in BDSM if they're competing for the attention of a submissive or a dominant. They might try to present their best side or, if that doesn't work, telling a little white lie or two about their experience might get them the attention they desire. Their slightly-elaborated presentations might get them the acceptance that they're looking for where their more actual and ordinary selves may not.

More extreme are the people who don't just try to convince the world that they're a little bit shinier or a little bit better than they are, but they instead try to convince themselves that they are as well. In their BDSM world, they might convince themselves that they like more pain than they do, or that flogging is more exciting for them than it really is, or that they love tying or being tied up more than they actually do. They might convince themselves that having their partner crawling at their feet is the right way for them to go when, in reality, they would be much better off the other way around. The motivations to do this creative self-deception can come from all sorts of sources. For example, the misplaced dominant I just mentioned might have been brought up in a family where he or she was exhorted to step out into the world and take charge of his or her life. It might simply not enter their mind that being submissive would be better for them.

Regardless of how such a false self comes into existence, when it's there it has a very big impact on engagement. What your partner does with you, how they behave and how they react, is going to be based on what they think you are and what they think you need. If they have the wrong idea then everything they do is going to be based on this wrong idea and will never completely hit the mark.

Likewise, if you're not being totally honest with yourself then you could easily be looking for the wrong thing for yourself. Our non-dominant from two paragraphs back is an ideal example of this. Convinced that they are (or should be) a great dominant and have submissives aplenty crawling at their feet, he or she may be constantly setting themselves up for relationships which never work out because they should be the one on the floor, not their partner.

All of what I am talking about here has to do with engagement which doesn't quite connect. It leads to dissatisfaction, sometimes niggling dissatisfaction like sand in your shoes, and sometimes to profound dissatisfaction of the "What the hell am I doing here?" type. Engagement is only going to work when you and your partner are engaging your real selves—not just at a superficial level, but deep down. The most technically excellent flogging is not going to be completely satisfying if it's not aimed at the right person for it. Dominating your partner and putting them in their place means you have to know exactly the right place to put them. If you don't know the real them, then you don't know their real place. And when you want to stand over your partner it has to really be you that's standing over them, not just someone wearing your body.

In sum, this engagement problem can occur a few different ways:

- We can have the wrong idea about ourselves,

- Our partner can have the wrong idea about us,

- We can have the wrong idea about our partner,

- Our partner can have the wrong idea about themselves, or

- Any combination of the above.

*The False Self*

A lot of the time this can come from not knowing ourselves, and then from communicating our uncertainties or wrong ideas to our partners.

It can also come from wishful thinking, such as excessively hoping that this vision of BDSM delight before us actually is a good fit for what we need. When we don't know this for sure and are filling in the gaps in our knowledge about this person with our own imagination, then what we end up engaging is going to be partly our own imagination instead of the real person, and this will certainly not be satisfying for them.

Regardless of where the wrong ideas come from, when you are actually in a BDSM relationship with someone, engaging them and interacting with the real them is vital to satisfaction and to the success of the relationship. Without this reality, what you do and share with them will not be completely satisfying. All your efforts and all their efforts will be focussed on the wrong things.

There's a key difference here between vanilla relationships and BDSM relationships. As I noted in book one, BDSM relationships are more about doing *to* your partner while vanilla relationships can be more about doing *with*. In vanilla relationships there is often much less need for engagement. If you go to the movies with your vanilla partner, or to a fine restaurant, or if you go para-sailing together, there isn't that same need to engage as there is in a dungeon. In vanilla, it can be enough that you both enjoy the activities you are sharing together. In BDSM—at least to have an actual relationship with your BDSM partner—you must be doing to, not just with. And to do to, you need to know your partner, what triggers them, how they respond, and so on.

# Chapter 3

# Trust

Trust has a number of aspects, but in terms of relationships the main thing which trust can effect is engagement.

Trust is sometimes superficially thought of as simply doing what you say you'll do, but it's not just about showing up on time for appointments or respecting your partner's use of their safeword. It's more about consistency and predictability. Your BDSM play partner can still have the deepest respect and trust for you even though you show up 15 minutes late for every single appointment, quite possibly because you are consistent.

This sort of trust is about you and your partner knowing how you each respond in a range of situations (and not just the ones where things go smoothly). When the going gets tough and your partner heads out the door, you aren't going to be able to trust that they'll be there for you during the hard times. That means that you won't expose yourself as much to them, you won't do anything particularly challenging with them, and that you'll keep your own barriers up more. The chance of them actually engaging all of the real you drops accordingly.

On the other hand, when they are reliable and when they do make an effort to do their best for both you and the relationship when things are difficult, shocking, or just plain hard, then you open yourself up more and there's increasingly better engagement.

Even in the face of good intentions and a commitment to do the best they can, trust can be hard to come by if they're inconsistent or unpredictable. If their priorities constantly change—perhaps due to work—or when the decisions they make affecting the relationship and you are constantly being influenced by external factors, you begin to perceive them as inconsistent and you can't trust them as much as you might otherwise.

Of course, when I'm talking about your partner I am also talking about you. For your partner to be able to trust you, to open themselves up, and to allow you to see the real them, you need to be consistent. When there are external factors—such as work or family—which conflict with your ability to commit and to be consistent—then your partner is going to limit their trust in you.

## 3.1  False self

Following on from my earlier discussion of false selves and their effect on engagement, we need to add trust into the mix because it's one of the things which determines both how much of our true selves we show to our partners and what sort of false self we might construct in their regard.

That last bit of the last paragraph is quite important. When we don't trust someone and we still want to be with them then we *may* create a false self which we present to them. For example, a dominant who finds mentally dominating a partner to be quite profound and intense may end up hiding this aspect of himself if he is with a submissive partner who is more into physical domination. He may find when he tries to mentally dominate her that she doesn't respond, doesn't even recognise what's happening, and may even make light of it. This might be painful for him, humiliating (in a bad way), or even embarrassing. In future, he might hide this part of himself either in similar situations or with similar submissives and this means that he has actually created a false self, one which he can display to these people, which is safe for him. In other words, this false self doesn't have an interest in mental domination, even though his real self does, and this false self is a way of protecting himself in situations where his passion for mental domination is not going to be appreciated.

There are two aspects to the sort of trust which I'm talking about here:

1. How much we trust our partner, and

2. How much we trust ourselves.

When we don't fully trust our partner, when we have doubts about whether they will accept us in all our kinky glory, this is when a false self starts to creep into existence. Instead of showing them our real selves, we show them an edited excerpt, with some bits of ourselves hidden away, and maybe with some extra bits which we don't really think or feel but which we hope will go down well with our partner.

Whether we don't trust our partner because of something they've done or haven't done, whether we don't trust them because of how previous partners have behaved, or whether we're simply afraid to trust doesn't matter. When they don't see the real us, they can't engage the real us.

The level of trust we require can be very deep. When we meet someone in vanilla-land who we really like, even talking about an occasional spanking risks potential rejection by them. If this person is someone we meet at a BDSM party, telling them we like spanking is not going to be a problem, but telling them that we like being dangled from meat-hooks by our nipples might be. And even if they are into what we might call a heavier side of BDSM, imagine that you find it immensely satisfying to have carrots which are hand-carved into the shape of religious icons inserted into your rectum, or that the most exciting bondage scenes for you are when your bottom is made up like Chucky from Child's Play and where you dangle them upside down and torture them with badly-played violin solos. How much trust is needed to let these cats out of the bag?

The trust we're talking about here is trusting that we will be accepted, that our partner won't suddenly become our ex-partner and run off into the distance screaming hysterically, and that they won't think less of us.

If we don't trust ourselves we can be saying we don't trust that what we are is sufficient or adequate to attract or keep our partner. It may well be that with a few tweaks to our behaviour or to our looks our partner will be hooked, but what is the price of this? If we need to behave differently than how we really feel because of our own doubts about ourselves then we are beginning to architect a false self to present to our partner and to the world, and as we've already discussed this leads to unsatisfying BDSM.

Again, it comes down to acceptance, but this time it is acceptance of ourselves. If posterially-inserted, hand-crafted carrots is the way you need to go and you convince yourself that it's just too kinky (or plain weird), you aren't accepting yourself. Settling for some easy rope play, a bit of slapping around, and then some basic horizontal hula is OK sometimes, but if you find yourself getting hot under the collar passing a grocery store and you don't do anything about it then you are denying both you and your partner some deep and possibly quite rewarding experiences.

## 3.2 Superficiality

One type of behaviour which is sure to trigger trust and false self problems is being superficial. This applies from both sides of a relationship.

As we've seen throughout this series of books, there are often powerful, intimate, and sometimes hidden motivations involved in our desires or needs for BDSM. While it may be about a bit of fun, relieving boredom, or about hotter sex some of the time for some people, believing that what we ourselves feel is only light-and-fluffy, or assuming that what our partner is feeling is just light-and-fluffy, may be avoiding real and profound needs.

When there are serious or profound needs involved which you don't communicate to your partner for whatever reason, then you are creating a false self for them to see. This false self doesn't have these profound needs. If all you are comfortable showing your partner is a happy-go-lucky BDSM fan then as far as your partner is concerned your profound needs don't exist and, therefore, they're not going to make any effort to help you satisfy them.

In addition, if all you're prepared to accept is that BDSM is just a bit of fun, or that it's just a bit of slap-and-tickle involving fluffy handcuffs, then your partner isn't going to show you any more than that because they know that you either don't understand or that you can't cope with anything more serious.

Even if BDSM is light-and-fluffy all of the time for you, it may not be for your partner and you need to be ready and open to accepting that.

# 3.3 Expectations

Trust is also about fulfilling our partner's expectations. We might create some of these expectations ourselves through what we say or do. For example, we might always be 10 minutes late for any appointment. While you could argue that our partner might then not be able to trust us to show up punctually, they still do know *consistently* when we'll show up and they'll be able to base what they do on that certainty. This certainty, even if it is that we'll always show up late, that we're hopeless with knots, or that we get bored with wax play, is what works to create trust, to let our partner drop their defences, display their real selves and to let us truly engage the real them.

Our partners will sometimes have their own expectations of us which we don't know about and which will influence how much they feel they can trust us. Their own expectations will come from the way they think things should be, not just with us, but often with anyone. This can be a problem with people new to BDSM because they don't know how BDSM or BDSM relationships really are and they may have ideas more inspired by the fantasy novels of Anne Rice than by reality.

The big tool for managing expectations is communication, about which I have more to say in the next chapter. Sitting down with your partner and discussing all the things you do together in fine detail can help reveal unrealistic expectations and create realistic expectations. For you both to be happy, expectations—both of what you and your partner are going to do and what you're not going to do—need to be met.

# Chapter 4

# Communication

In almost all cases, communication plays a key role in relationship problems—both in creating the problems in the first place, and then in resolving them. Communication is a major topic and I can't hope to completely do it justice here, but I'd like to at least touch on some areas to do with communication problems to highlight the sorts of things we BDSMers can face.

One of the first things to realise about communication between two people is that it's never, ever going to be perfect. For a start, when we try to talk to someone we may have an idea or image in our minds which we want to transfer to theirs but the means we have to do this basically come down to words and gestures. We might have a great plan for some suspension bondage and in our mind we can imagine the texture of the rope, the clanking of the winch as we hoist our partner into the air, the smell of sweat and fear emanating from them, the pattern of rope and knots which we have laid out across their body, the colour changes in their skin where the rope and knots begin to press in, and so forth. But regardless of what we say, be it, "I want to tie you up and dangle you from on high," or be it something more colourful like my description earlier in this paragraph, the words we say may not conjure up in our partner's mind exactly what we are thinking. And even if we were the most skilled writer or poet in the world, words will never exactly express what we think.

This means, of course, that there's room for misinterpretation. Our partner might think A when we mean B. We might mean we're going to do this suspension out in a forest, and they might have in mind that it's going to happen in a private dungeon space. We might be thinking of using rough hemp rope and they might be thinking of something softer, like cotton. We might be thinking of this scene as a 30-minute warm-up before some energetic, hot-n'-horny horizontal action, and they might be thinking of it more as a 2-hour tranquil meditation followed by a quick nap and then some coffee.

Engagement can also enter into the discussion here. If what we know about our partner is just what they'd like us to think— i.e., when they show us a false self of some sort—then when we talk to them to explain our ideas and visions, the words we choose are going to be aimed at that false self, not at their real self. We all know from experience that what we say to someone can be misinterpreted, and we all learn to adapt what we say to the person we're saying it to. We do this so that they have a better chance of getting the right message. We choose the words which we think are right for that particular person. If we were to try to communicate the same idea to a different person we might use different words. We adapt our communication style and choices from person to person. But, when we don't really know the person we're talking to, or when what we know about them is not quite true or is incomplete, then the words we choose will not be right. There's a greater chance that this other person will get the wrong idea of what we mean.

Communication also acquires its own BDSM-specific problems which we need to recognise. In particular, one of the pillars of BDSM—namely disparity of power—often means that communication becomes one-sided. One way this manifests is when a submissive or slave relinquishes authority to their partner. Along with this, they may think that they relinquish the right to comment on or be critical about the things they have relinquished authority over. So, for example, a submissive who lets their dominant decide how a rope scene should play out is often more reticent to comment during a scene than, say, a bottom who hasn't relinquished any authority and who retains the idea that both they and their partner have equal say in what goes on.

For a slave or submissive in this situation, their reluctance to communicate can be:

- Because they don't want to be seen as stepping on the authority they have handed over,

- Because they don't want to feel like they are taking over control,

- Because they don't want to appear to be interfering or meddling, or

- Because they don't think it is their right to comment any more.

One case of this I came across was when a submissive woman contacted me about a conflict she was experiencing. She was deeply committed to serving, obeying, and being useful to her master but she was finding that her own needs weren't being met. She felt that it was not her place to be any sort of burden on her master. She only wanted to serve and be useful, and to her it seemed that it wasn't her place to be looking for him to satisfy her own needs when it should be she who was satisfying his. As a result, she was experiencing significant conflict. On the one hand she felt it inappropriate to talk to him about these needs, while on the other hand she had these same serious needs which weren't being addressed.

Another difficulty can be with a master and slave where the slave is only allowed to speak at certain times and in certain ways. Clearly, in such a situation communication is constrained and this increases the chance that problems or issues, which might otherwise be aired, remain unspoken, then fester, then break out in a burst of unpleasantness.

The above examples are of situations which generally don't exist in vanilla-land, except perhaps in the military. These communication problems, or potential problems, crop up due to the exercise of disparate power and we need to take steps to mitigate them without compromising our ability to use, experience and enjoy power.

Here are a few ideas:

- If you are a master with a slave who you keep under speech restrictions most of the time, set aside regular periods—maybe one hour once per week—where they can speak their mind without fear of punishment. Alternatively, allow them to request to "speak freely" along the lines of the military. However, to preserve authority do make it clear that at these times you only guarantee to listen, not to change your mind or do what they want.

- Similarly, when you are a submissive or slave and you want to express a desire but also don't want to feel that you're pushing or trying to tell your partner what to do, try agreeing that whatever you say is just information for your partner and that it's up to them whether they act on it or not.

- Have a journal in which you write everything down and keep it in a known place for your partner to read when you're not around.

- Leave notes where your partner will find them.

More generally, communication problems are often standard problems which exist just as much in vanilla-land as they do in BDSM-land and which require the same sorts of strategies to solve or prevent:

- Don't assume that your partner will work out, know, or guess something. Ideally, when you don't tell your partner something they need to know they'll ask you about it, but if they don't know that you've left something out—such as the fact that you already have another submissive, that you're allergic to nylon rope, or that you have no visual depth perception when you are proposing to use a single-tail whip on them—then they may not ask and things might go askew.

- Send each other email... even if you live together.

- If there are certain activities during a scene which you feel embarrassed requesting, agree on a set of signals beforehand so that you don't actually have to say the words.

- When you explain something to your partner, get them to explain whatever it is back to you to make sure they understood.

- Keep in mind that a lot of communication is non-verbal. Facial expressions and gestures add to the message, such as having your arms crossed while talking usually indicates either that you're feeling defensive or that you're not being open.

  Facial expressions and gestures are missing completely during telephone calls, SMS and email, and so you need to be particularly careful when using these mediums to make sure the right message gets across.

- Lots of people have unconscious drives which might be conflicting with their conscious ones and this can make communication confusing. Fear, in particular, is often a culprit here.

It is always better to say something than to say nothing. I have come across some tops and dominants who don't talk with their partner because they feel that it takes away from their authority. Or, if they have strong feelings or emotions, they feel it weakens them to display these emotions to their submissive.

It might be fine to not tell your partner what you're about to do in a scene so as to create suspense or to surprise them. It also might be fine to not talk to them about some things simply because they don't need to know, such as that you had to throw one of your many floggers away because all the tails fell out. But, they do need to know about things that affect you, them, or the relationship because these have to do with engagement. If you don't communicate with them about these things then engagement suffers and you create distance.

I'd like to return to the submissive I mentioned earlier, the one who felt it was her place to serve and be useful, and not be a burden to her master to such an extent that she felt it wrong to tell him about her own needs. I gave her a car analogy. If you are service-oriented and think that being a burden on your master or asking him for something is inappropriate, then consider a car. A car needs fuel and regular maintenance, and this is something we all accept. A car without maintenance will eventually stop providing service. When the fuel gauge needle points to "E" or the fuel warning light starts flashing, it isn't the case that the car is begging for fuel, or that it is whining or whinging, or even that it is demanding that we put fuel in it. The warning signal which our car gives us is neutral communication, and if you're strongly service-oriented then you can think of what you say to your master the same way. You let them know the state of things, warn them of imminent problems with your service. Then you let them deal with it. The same as in a car, if the fuel runs out in spite of a warning from the fuel gauge, the car owner needs to deal with it. When you regard yourself as property and if you have a need which doesn't get met in spite of warnings to your master, then it's his problem to deal with it.

# Chapter 5

# Surrender versus submission

Surrender is vital to being able to fully experience something. If you are busy standing by the "experience door" waiting for the time—which may or may not come—when you decide to close the door because you've had enough, then you'll never be able to fully experience what happens to you. Part of you will always be detached and devoting itself to acting as doorkeeper. Not all of you will be available to actually *feel*.

Needing to act as a doorkeeper is not necessarily a bad thing in some situations, but it is a problem when you want to fully immerse yourself in your BDSM. For example, when you have a well-developed set of skills and are flogging a very experienced partner, then you can pretty much go to town knowing that they are capable, competent, and are going to do the right thing.

Likewise, if your partner is carving designs into your upper arm and you know and trust them and their skills completely, you can surrender yourself to the experience and just let go.

But if you are doing something with someone and don't know their skill level, or you don't know how they'll handle intensity or potential difficulties, or if you just don't know them well enough to fully trust them, then you submit to what they're doing instead of surrendering, and you make sure that part of you is standing aside and is consciously keeping track of what they're doing.

When you are in a relationship with someone and you find yourself holding back during play, or you find you are limiting yourself in some particular aspects of the relationship, particularly where D&s is concerned, then perhaps you're having trouble surrendering. As I mentioned, trust can be part of this. Importantly, it may be that your partner is doing everything right and that it's something in you that is preventing full surrender on your part. Maybe it's something from your past, or maybe it's because you are entering BDSM territory which is confronting or for which you're not ready.

The difference between surrender and submission when engaging in something is typically this doorkeeper aspect. Surrender is the giving up of yourself completely either to your partner or to the experience you are having. Submission is when you leave yourself a way out beyond that which happens naturally.

Surrender is vital to penetration, to feeling or experiencing your partner, and to getting the most out of what you do together. There are many reasons why surrender doesn't happen, or why some people consciously or unconsciously avoid surrender.

- Some see surrender as an indication that they're weak or that it makes them vulnerable. Well, being vulnerable is the purpose of surrender! Actually fully opening yourself—whether you are a top, bottom, dominant, submissive, etc.—is critical to getting the most out of your BDSM. If you put up barriers to surrendering then the most profound experiences will pass you by.

- When trust or fear are factors, my experience suggests that it's mostly:

    - Because you don't trust yourself,
    - Because you are afraid of how you might change if you do surrender,
    - Because of a fear of losing control,
    - Because of a fear of finding out something about yourself that you have been keeping hidden away, or
    - Because your partner might discover or see something in you that you have been trying to keep hidden.

- It could also be that you don't trust your partner. You may not trust them to respect and be gentle with what you reveal when you do surrender. You also may know that they're a stupid asshole and will deal with your surrender poorly. They may be an unstoppable gossip and you need to keep some sensitive parts of you private. From a purely physical perspective they may have really bad aim and letting them loose on your ass with a cane is never going to end well, or they always tie knots too tightly, and so on.

- Some people engage an archetype or an imagined figure in their mind during scenes instead of engaging, and being penetrated by, their partner. This is a way of avoiding surrendering. What they are surrendering to is an image in their mind, but it's in their mind (which they control!) and so it is not really surrender at all. Eventually, the thrill will fade and the person doing it may end up dissatisfied and go looking for a new partner without realising that they themselves were at fault.

# Chapter 6

# Dominance and submission

Dominance involves claiming authority over, and then controlling or directing, your submissive partner. Complementally, submission is about relinquishing authority and surrendering yourself to the control and direction of your partner. In book two of this series I listed a number of areas in which you can assert control over a submissive such as directing their sensations, controlling their emotions, inflicting pain on them, restricting their movement, directing how they serve, reducing their sense of identity, and so on.

D&s is a tool we can use to engage and penetrate our partners. As I've noted elsewhere, experiencing control—whether it is being controlled or being the one doing the controlling—is a common motivator in BDSM and can be quite powerful. It can be what is behind many of our BDSM activities such as flogging or bondage, and making it a focus can enhance our BDSM.

D&s also has its potential problems, pitfalls and obstacles. They fall into two main areas:

- Controlling things which shouldn't be controlled, and

- Not controlling things which should be controlled.

# 6.1   The knight in shining armour

Almost by definition a dominant likes to take control or to be in control. They can feel uncomfortable when they're not. This leads to a significant trap, namely thinking that you can solve your submissive's problems by taking control. You might be tempted to do so because:

- Your submissive seems indecisive,

- They seem easily mislead and fall prey to others, or

- You have more knowledge and experience than they do.

You may think that everything will be more wonderful once you take over.

This is you being a knight-in-shining-armour saving a damsel-in-distress. Unfortunately, many such damsels merely look good. Often, they are constantly in distress and constantly need saving[1]. What you may end up doing is burdening yourself with someone who is chronically either unable or unwilling to take care of themselves. They aren't going to "get better" under your attentions, and what you might be walking into is a relationship with a submissive who has specifically set out to find someone who will take responsibility for their lives. This is a very bad place to be. You end up enabling them to continue to be immature and to avoid responsibility.

Some people think that a submissive or slave is that way because they want someone to take charge and make all the decisions. To a limited extent this is true, but personal responsibility tends to increase for a slave or submissive when they enter into a relationship with a master or dominant rather than decrease. This is because to be of use to their partner they first need to be handling their own lives well, and then they can serve their partner. This means that they already shoulder the responsibility of caring for themselves and then take on additional responsibility given to them by their dominant partner. The responsibility they carry goes up, rather than down, when they are in a relationship with a dominant.

In terms of penetration, this additional responsibility is something the submissive or slave can feel. Indeed, for some slaves and submissives, this form of penetration or feeling can be what they want or crave from their BDSM.

A "slave" or "submissive" who consciously or unconsciously heaps their own crap onto their dominant partner becomes a burden to their dominant and is actually using their dominant

---

[1] I don't want to suggest that it's only women who play the part of the perennially-distressed damsel in need of saving. Some so-called submissive guys can also play the same part just as well as women, or better.

to serve them rather than the other way around. Some of these "vampire submissives" are very skilled at sucking the life out of dominants and oftentimes the dominants don't recognise what is happening. These submissives are, to put it kindly, poorly adapted to being a submissive. It is not a dominant's job to fix or repair a submissive. It might be a dominant's job to give their submissive advice or training, but being a crutch is not.

Just as BDSM can appear superficially attractive to those who are simply looking for opportunities to harm others because it's "obviously" about pain, BDSM can also appear attractive to those who don't want to take responsibility for themselves because it's "obviously" about people (i.e., submissives) not taking responsibility for themselves and letting dominants take charge.

So for a dominant it's important to tread very carefully in any areas of personal responsibility of your submissive. How they take care of themselves, their work, their financial future, and their medical needs are areas of personal responsibility. While there can be some very difficult choices to make in all of these areas at different times of our lives, unless you're looking at long-term profound ownership it's unlikely that you should be making decisions in any of these areas for your submissive. On the other hand, training and education as it impacts your goals for them, what they do on a day-to-day basis, and specific instructions regarding their behaviour can be entirely yours and rightly so.

For a submissive it's important to manage responsibility so that you are a support, rather than a burden to your dominant or master. Particularly when your dominant is more experienced than you, or more mature, or more intelligent, it can be tempting to lean too much on their decision-making ability, and being decisive can certainly be a highly attractive and natural ability in some dominants. However, both for dominants and submissives, a BDSM relationship—or any relationship, actually—is an opportunity to grow, rather than shrink, and if you find yourself or your world becoming smaller instead of larger due to the nature of your relationship with your partner then you should do something about it.

## 6.2   Dominance or submission as duty

Just as much as control sometimes shouldn't be asserted or claimed, at other times it should be. There is often an implicit understanding between a dominant and a submissive that the dominant will dominate and that the submissive will submit. This sounds obvious, but many D&s folk get together more because of their personalities, their hopes, and their dreams rather than their abilities to actually and actively dominate or submit. Let me clarify this: if a guy meets a girl, gets her in the sack, and demonstrates amazing vigour, she might be quite impressed. If she's particularly randy on an ongoing basis she might think that this guy can satisfy her clitoral and vaginal needs on an ongoing basis as well. However, maybe he just came off an extended dry period and being that vigorous was a one-off performance. Maybe, as he gets acclimatised to the increased attention his dick receives his vigour trails off and she finds herself unsatisfied.

The same can apply to D&s. When a dominant and a submissive set up shop together it is because they have BDSM wants or needs which they want to satisfy within that relationship. There can be an expectation that this will occur. Because it takes the two of them to make this happen, if one looses steam and the

D&s or BDSM stops happening then the other may quite rightly feel poorly done by.

In casual BDSM encounters, say at a party, this problem doesn't exist, but for each person in a long-term relationship helping to ensure their partner's needs are met probably should rise to the level of being a duty or obligation. If one partner starts running out of puff, they should talk about this and work together to find a solution.

In book two of this series I listed a number of ways in which dominance and submission can be experienced and expressed—such as hunter/prey, emotional, service, intellectual domination, etc. When reviewing a D&s relationship and what makes it tick, it's vital to recognise that there is probably more than one type of domination involved and it may well be that a combination of D&s styles is necessary. If one partner runs out of energy for one style it may not be sufficient to throw more energy into other styles to make up for it. Each style or each D&s activity may serve to satisfy particular needs and may not be easily replaceable with other styles.

# 6.3   Losing control is easy

Many of the pitfalls of D&s relationships are particularly relevant to the dominant and can be quite easy for the dominant to fall into. Mostly they have to do with us not taking control when we should. This is perhaps related to it often being the case that the dominant needs to take the initiative and actively claim control. Sometimes we don't notice the times or opportunities for us to do this and they slip us by.

Here are a few notes on the subject:

*Dominance and submission*

- Your submissive partner is not wanting or expecting your orders or directions to be a reflection of their own wants or needs. This is perhaps an easy trap to fall into. Your partner probably didn't sign up to a D&s relationship with you because you'd do what they wanted. It should be the other way around—i.e., that they'd do what you want—but in moments of difficulty or doubt it can be surprisingly easy to slip into a mode of thought where making your partner happy by doing nice things to them seems the way to go.

- D&s is not about your submissive having it easy. That's not to say that they shouldn't find their relationship with you satisfying and rewarding. But if the direction you set for them involves them often eating chocolate or cake, getting frequent orgasms, being dressed up how they like, going to parties and doing things they enjoy, having coffee with friends, socialising with other like-minded folk, and so on, then you're not really dominating them. It's more a case of you kowtowing to their desires, whether they're spoken or not.

- Your submissive partner should experience some discomfort and resistance in being your submissive. Again, this doesn't mean that they don't have a good and rewarding time. But, if what you have them do is what they'd do anyway—such as if you have them bring you a coffee when they quite enjoy doing things for you—then you're not dominating them at all. For you to dominate, you need to be in command, using your authority and control over them to get your way. They need to feel this, and so do you. This is penetration and, as we've seen, this is a vital part of BDSM. Your partner needs to deeply feel your control over them. If you push them and they easily move in the direction you have set then it probably means that neither of you will feel very penetrated, but if you move in a more challenging direction and there's resistance and you overcome it then the penetration will be much more.

- Your partner—and you—need you to not just be in charge, but to actually use the authority you have. If you use your authority merely to tell them to eat a piece of chocolate— which they'd quite happily do anyway—or to tell them to go to the dungeon and undress when they're ready to do so anyway, then you're not commanding. At most, you're simply giving them a good idea.

## 6.4 Opportunities to control

Keep your submissive on their toes so that both you and your submissive are aware of your authority. Even when out in public, or with vanilla friends or family members you can still maintain the control. Make clear to your partner beforehand that when you ask them to do something that it is to be taken as a command and prompt obedience is expected—e.g., to refill your glass, to look up something on the computer, or to serve food to you and others in a formal or semi-formal manner. You can also establish non-verbal signals (which are particularly useful at parties, whether they are BDSM or vanilla parties) so that your partner needs to keep you in sight in case you signal them. Table 6.1 on the facing page has some example signals you might use.

Remember that an important aspect of this is penetration. You and your partner need to feel this control, and in the case of

| Action | Meaning |
|---|---|
| Rock your glass from side to side | "Get me a refill for my drink." |
| Rub your chin | "It's time to leave. Fetch our coats and bags." |
| Rub your upper arm with your other hand | If at a play party: "I want to play now. Get ready. Collect our equipment and move it into the dungeon." |
| Lightly slap your own knee | "Come and sit at my feet." |
| Brush the hair on the back of your head with your hand | "Bring me something to eat." |

Table 6.1: Party D&s signals

party signals the penetration comes both from your submissive needing to be constantly alert to what you're doing so that they're ready to respond immediately, and from you seeing them respond to your signal.

You can get similar results when you require your submissive to always walk on one particular side when you are out and about, or to only start eating a meal once you have started, or to not climb into bed until you're already in bed, etc. These all require your submissive to be attentive to what you're doing and thus feel control.

This isn't a free ride though because you have to keep in mind that what you do can't frustrate your control over your submissive or slave. You need to ensure that there are opportunities for, and no obstructions to, their obedience. For example, you can't tell a submissive to always walk on your left and then go shopping in stores with very narrow aisles and expect your submissive to be where she should.

Likewise, you also need to be attentive that they are doing what they should. You shouldn't let infractions slip by uncorrected. You can't just give orders once and then think that your job is done. The penetration side of BDSM involves you penetrating your submissive ongoing. If you just give an order once and then don't follow up, your partner only gets penetrated by you that one time.

# 6.5   Conclusion

When we compare scene-based BDSM, such as flogging or bondage, to D&s we might note that it's easy to recognise the penetration occurring in a scene because we can see the submissive writhing or flinching and the dominant feeding off that. This penetration is often quite tangible. But in D&s penetration is often more subtle or restrained and is often felt for much longer than in a scene. Because it is more subtle it can be harder to notice when it starts to fade or when it starts losing its penetrating power.

It's important to keep in mind that it is often this penetrative aspect which is the most important for a satisfying and rewarding D&s relationship rather than the simple fact or nature of any orders.

# Chapter 7

# Wrong reasons why people do BDSM

A quick first glance at BDSM suggests that it's all about pain and sex. Because of this, it has a peculiar fascination for what we might call the wrong sort of people. These include those who carry a lot of anger around with them, the socially desperate, the excessively horny, the sociopathically inclined, and the immature. These folk often don't get into BDSM to have a healthy, intimate, personally-rewarding and mutually-beneficial relationship with a partner. Instead, they get into BDSM as a way of selfishly using any potential partners they meet.

## 7.1 Unattractive and looking to get laid

Some people are unattractive. This could be because of their looks, their lack of fitness, their weight, their body odour, their ego, their allergy to soap, their personality, or their attitude towards others and life in general. Consequently, finding a partner relying on their own merits is unlikely to be successful. These socially desperate souls can get the idea that picking up a flogger or baring their back are acceptable ways to get laid. This might actually work for a while, but it's a hollow win.

Unfortunately, it can be a successful strategy because in some geographical areas there can be a surplus of tops and dominants and a lack of bottoms or submissives, or *vice versa*. When there is such a shortfall, pretending that you are available and able to fill the gap can make you attractive to people who have no better alternative.

Pretending to be into some BDSM activity when you're not is, naturally enough, a bad idea. Firstly, it reduces your own self-image or feelings of self-worth in an unhealthy way[1]. It's also dishonest. It's a strategy for deceiving a potential partner into providing sex or affection or both without providing them the actual BDSM they thought they would get.

The better solutions to finding a bed- or dungeon-mate include fitness clubs, deodorant, shaving, a good diet, and perhaps most important of all, some serious attitude readjustment. In many cases, socially desperate folk are lazy, and their choice of simply

---

[1] Note that BDSM can include healthy and constructive humiliation as a form of play, but this is very different to what we're talking about here.

*Wrong reasons why people do BDSM*

making themselves available BDSM-wise is a way to avoid having to do any hard work on themselves.

Spotting these pretenders straight away can be a challenge because they've almost certainly been playing their particular deceiving game for a while and may have developed some skill at getting away with it.

Be wary of someone who claims to be into BDSM but who:

1. Tries to get the BDSM over with and get into sex as soon as possible, or

2. Shows no interest in either developing their BDSM skill, or in working with you to improve the scenes you do together.

Sad, really.

## 7.2  Sociopathic and looking to hurt someone

Sociopaths do exist. They are looking for someone to genuinely hurt or to take advantage of. They are usually quite slick and well-presented, and they seem to say and do all the right things. This is an act, and they need to be good at it because they're trying to draw you in to their own twisted reality while making it seem like the best thing since sliced bread. What they seem to be offering though, turns out to be shallow or have no value to you. They often don't care about or dismiss your feelings.

BDSM can be attractive to sociopaths because it seems—superficially—to be about hurting people and this is what sociopaths live to do. If you're after pain without any consideration of your welfare, then hooking up with a sociopath is definitely the way to go. There's more to BDSM than simply inflicting pain of course, and we've seen that pain is actually a gateway to other experiences, with the pain being a means to useful, satisfying and productive outcomes rather than being an end in itself.

Sociopaths can confuse you. They may play on your ignorance or your need to please. They may say things like, "A real submissive would be able to take what I do!" or "You want to learn to be a good submissive, don't you?". Even though you may be hurt, confused, frustrated and suffering, they can make it seem like all the problems are your own fault or that everything is due to your own shortcomings.

A common clue that you're involved with such a person is fear. If you are constantly or frequently afraid—afraid of being hurt, afraid of not being able to please, afraid of not being good enough, afraid of doing the wrong thing—then it's time to go. If you don't genuinely look forward to the experiences you have with your partner then ditto. BDSM is not a matter of just one person getting their needs met.

# 7.3   Wanting an easy way to get sex

Candles, romantic dinners, and cosy evenings on a boat on the river with champagne and canapes are just too hard sometimes. For someone who is often just plain horny (i.e., a guy), it's far easier to dress up in black, collect a few ropes, and then show up at the next BDSM social event as Master Tie-Me-Up.

Tying someone up may be enough to get sex for a while, but it's poor BDSM. If the partner of such a person is actually looking for something deeper then it's not going to be there.

There's a lot of overlap with this bad reason for doing BDSM and someone doing BDSM because they think they're unattractive. They're both manipulative and dishonest. They're also selfish and shallow. Unfortunately, some people who are enthusiastic about actual, real, genuine BDSM get sucked in by these false presentations and eventually get spat out.

Just as with the unattractive folk, the clue here is that the person you're dealing with has no interest in developing or exploring their BDSM experience or yours. They're only interested in doing as much BDSM as necessary to get into your pants.

# 7.4   Wanting a fashion accessory

A variation on this is the person who is looking to hook up with someone they think is attractive so they can then show them off as a sort of fashion accessory. This happens on both sides of BDSM—some submissives will try to connect with a desirable top or dominant who they can then present to their friends at parties, and some tops and dominants will try to find an attractive submissive or bottom who they can then have on a leash or at their feet at BDSM social events.

This becomes a problem when their focus on showing you off gets in the way of satisfying and enjoyable BDSM. If you go to BDSM social events with the expectation that there'll be socializing and play, and you find your partner is exceptionally keen on you dressing up and then doesn't play with you then it's perhaps time for a little chat.

# 7.5 Angry and no other way to get rid of the anger

There are many pissed off people in the world. They could be angry with their bosses, with the way the world seems to be treating them, because they think they should have a life or circumstances better than they do, because they're ineffectual, or even because they have psychological problems. They may just carry anger around with them 24 hours a day.

When they're angry they want to take it out on someone. BDSM can be attractive for this because it can seem to be mainly about hitting people a lot. Using a pretence of BDSM to express their anger isn't going to help these angry people in the long term. In particular, they may come to think that all of their partners are there to be hit and this is, of course, a bad thing. Being angry isn't a good reason to be involved BDSM.

Having said that it's important to clarify something. Being angry 24 hours a day is not a good reason to search out someone to flog, whip, or cane. But when the underlying BDSM relationship is one of caring and support, then it can be a genuine service by a slave or submissive to hand their dominant a cane or flogger and bare their back or buttocks so that their partner can work out any temporary frustration on them. There are good benefits to this. Firstly, it provides a safe outlet to the top or dominant for their emotions. Secondly, it is a genuine opportunity for their submissive or slave to provide a useful service. Thirdly, they are both supporting each other in the context of their relationship with each other.

Two things are important about this latter scenario:

1. It is honest and open, and

2. It's only safely applicable when the emotions being released through the flogging or caning are temporary or occasional. Constant anger or frustration is a reason to seriously look at your life, or to find a professional to help you manage this anger.

## 7.6 Revenge

For some people there are times when they think that they have been treated badly, are angry about it, and seek revenge.

It may well be that the person who feels this way has legitimate cause, but it might also be that they themselves are the major contributor to their frustration. For example, a submissive might have gone into a BDSM relationship with their dominant partner knowing that there were some firm limits involved—such as their dominant having children and needing to work long hours to earn money to support them. When the submissive's needs grow and they need more time or attention from their dominant, they may become angry when their dominant has no more time to spare or when their dominant makes choices which don't place them, the submissive, above all else. This may seem obviously selfish, and this may well be a situation which was easy to foresee happening, but when hungers are aroused and feelings are strong, the submissive may not see it that way and may feel they are genuinely being treated poorly.

Choosing to take revenge is a choice made when there are no other choices, when the person involved doesn't have any other way of getting some compensation for a wrong they think they have experienced. It is a backdoor choice used when the front door isn't an option. Because of this, a sense of disempowerment can be involved with choosing to take revenge. The act of taking revenge can be felt as a way of taking back control.

Revenge often takes shape as some form of attack against which the person being attacked either has no defence or is unprepared. Because it's usually based on emotions, there may not be any rational or reasonable connection between the perceived wrong and the revenge taken. Anger, jealousy, and frustration are often the main motivators for revenge, and sometimes the acts of revenge can be extreme and irrevocable.

- The aggrieved person—the one seeking revenge—might target another relationship of the person who they think did them wrong so as to break up that relationship. For example, they might seduce the partner of the person who they think did them wrong simply to cause problems.

- They might target the health of the person they're pissed off with. In rare cases some have arranged for this person to get infected with something nasty, such as with Hepatitis or HIV. Sadly, university researchers have actually documented people doing this[2].

- They might go on a crusade to persecute this person and ruin their way of life. For example, they may engage in BDSM with them (with a smile, of course) and then report these BDSM activities to the police or "out" the person to their work colleagues or family.

- They also might cause damage to or steal the person's property. They could slash the tyres of their car, or spray graffiti on their house.

---

[2][MESTON2007]

Revenge often knows no logic and sometimes it can be incredibly patient. To avoid it, take the time to get to know any new partner before getting too involved with them. Try to avoid love (or BDSM) triangles. This can be difficult because many BDSM communities are quite small, and people moving from one partner to another is common.

The Internet has created additional opportunities for revenge. For example, a submissive who—rightly or wrongly—feels that she has been badly done by can join an on-line and international submissive support group and start spreading stories largely unchallenged because their target dominant isn't participating in the group. While I have no problem with someone talking about their bad experiences, there are always two sides to every story and using a forum where the other person concerned cannot reply is unfair (and is probably done for that very reason). But, revenge is very rarely fair.

It's worth noting that an imbalance of power is a requirement for BDSM, and that a submissive or slave is going to be in a position of less power than their partner. This may mean that a submissive is going to be more prone to considering revenge because fewer options are open to them.

# 7.7 Simply selfish

More generally, I suppose that doing BDSM for bad reasons is often about being selfish. Wanting something for yourself and using BDSM to get it is a bad motivation. For people who do this, it's about getting what they want and not being too concerned about the others who they trample on. Justification and rationalisation can play a part—these folk create excuses in their own mind which either justify what they're doing, or which somehow twist reality in their own mind to make it seem that their partners/victims deserve it or will thank them for it later.

This sort of relationship is one-way. They want from you but aren't prepared to give in return. They may say the right words, but it always seems that you're the one who is at fault by wanting things your way or by wanting your own needs met. At the same time, they make sure that their needs always are.

## 7.8 Misguided attempt to heal your partner

One of my other interests is hypnosis. My first book was about using hypnosis to enhance sex[3]. Because of this public interest of mine I was once approached by a dominant at a BDSM play party who came to talk to me about using hypnosis on his submissive female partner. She suffered from manic depression and was being treated by a psychiatrist for it. This well-meaning dominant wanted to use hypnosis on his partner to "cure" her. He wanted to know why he couldn't just hypnotise her and tell her to be happy all the time.

You can't use hypnosis, or BDSM, to heal your partner. If they have psychological, emotional, or psychiatric problems then leave these to people who have the qualifications and experience to treat them. Applying laymen's cures or trying to help can make things worse.

---

[3][MASTERS2008A]

With this we may be getting into an area where some dominants have a weakness. Some dominants really, really—and I mean REALLY—like, or even need to be in control. When things aren't under their control they can become uncomfortable. When some of us see our partners in difficulty we want to use our power and position in their lives to fix things even when it's not right to do so. We can feel compelled to act because we feel so uncomfortable not being in control any more. Doing something, even the wrong thing, can make us feel like we're back in the driver's seat again (albeit possibly in the driver's seat of a train on a one-way trip to a spectacular wreck!).

Some dominants get suckered into this situation deliberately by "submissives" who aren't submissive at all, but who are actually immature and don't want to accept responsibility (I also talked about this in *The knight in shining armour*, section 6.1 on page 32).

It's true that BDSM can sometimes be cathartic or provide opportunities for emotional expression and release. It can't cure though. Don't be tempted to try because you may end up with a submissive or slave who is more broken than when they met you.

## 7.9 Looking to solve a problem with BDSM when it's not BDSM-amenable

The above is a specific example of a much more general bad reason to do BDSM, and that is to try to use BDSM to solve a problem which has nothing to do with BDSM.

If by circumstance or by choice you're ugly or undesirable, then BDSM may provide a way for you to get laid. It's not a good use of BDSM if for no other reason than it doesn't make you feel good about yourself. If you have to fake or force an interest in BDSM to get laid then that's very sad and even demeaning. On top of that, it can mean misleading or taking advantage of someone who genuinely is looking for a BDSM partner.

Another bad reason someone might do BDSM is if they are emasculated in their everyday life—perhaps by a domineering supervisor at work, or because they're timid, or because they're afraid of confrontation and let people take advantage of them. They might try to make up for it by being dominant in the bedroom, or by wearing black leather and wielding the biggest flogger at every play party. This might make them temporarily feel better, but isn't a solution to the problem.

BDSM also often seems exciting to outsiders, and if someone feels their life is tedium *ad nauseum* then rather than work out what's gone wrong they instead do something exciting to fill the gap. This may be something like skydiving, insulting mafiosi, or trying BDSM. None of these solve the problem of a boring personality, and a genuinely uninteresting person can take the excitement out of anything, even out of being TASERed™.

Exploring BDSM is only a solution for BDSM-related problems. If you're genuinely hungry for someone to control you and having such a person in your life helps you grow and feel complete then chalk one up for BDSM. If an intense cutting scene is cathartic for you or helps you feel closer to your chosen partner then chalk another one up to BDSM. However, if you're a dickhead looking for excitement and you get involved in BDSM, then you end up still being a dickhead but now you have a flogger.

# 7.10   I will train you

BDSM—at least for newcomers—can be a tantalising world of strange, new, and powerful experiences. It can surprise and overwhelm, and it can be hard to know where to look or what to do. You can get lost in it.

This may be when Super Dom rides up on his black leather steed carrying a glistening array of floggers, nipple clamps, rope, candles and chain. "Follow me," he says, "and I will train you! I will show you the way to ecstasy unbounded. Your life will change immeasurably for the better and you will become my slave!"

Sadly though, sometimes what Super Dom says can be translated as, "Come with me, away from others who might know more than I, and then I will flog you and fuck you until you learn to enjoy it."

Ignorance is the problem here. The real nature of BDSM is not something which our society excels at teaching. As a result, many people enter into the world of BDSM with fantastic and unreal ideas about what to expect and about how BDSM folk really behave. A newcomer may be overwhelmed and hungry for more of what BDSM has to offer but be ignorant and ill-prepared for abusive dominants. These "dominants" might look the part and might have splashed out a couple of hundred dollars at the local leather store, but all they're doing is waiting for their chance to pick up some "fresh meat" which hasn't yet learned to recognise their true game.

Some of this—but not all of it—can be due to lack of experience and lack of imagination on the part of Super Dom combined with an overarching need on his part to get his dick wet. Super Dom may genuinely believe that all he needs is a couple of floggers and a pair of nipple clamps to bring on unlimited rapture in women because he saw another guy do it and it didn't look that hard.

Having such a "dominant" spoil your early BDSM experiences by making it about being physically abused and then being fucked repeatedly can take some of the shine off it for a new submissive.

This training game goes both ways. Super Subbie might also be lurking on BDSM websites or at parties looking for attention, and may latch on to an inexperienced top or dominant and offer to "teach" them. In reality, it could be a ploy to keep this "fresh meat" to themselves and get their own needs met—such as heavy floggings or bondage—while telling their victim that this is what all tops do for their submissives.

## The real thing

There are real teachers and trainers out there, and some of them do contribute their time and expertise to others largely out of the goodness of their hearts, so don't necessarily get turned off by what I wrote above.

Do keep in mind:

- Many people who will genuinely help you and provide training are involved with an organised and long-standing BDSM social group or club,

- Ethical teachers and trainers will have no problem with you asking around about their skill and *bona fides*, and

*Wrong reasons why people do BDSM*

- Ethical teachers and trainers will sometimes say no when they see a conflict of interest in helping you, or when they recognise that they're not what you need. They may refer you to others who have skills or knowledge better suited to where your interests lie.

Things to do:

- Recognise that your genitals may get in the way of you making sensible decisions,

- Make sure to ask around,

- Your first BDSM experiences are best had somewhere you feel safe, perhaps at a play party where you know some of the people, or when you have a friend riding chaperone.

## Questions

The following questions can help you separate the wheat from the chaff:

1. If someone is offering to teach you or coach you, what do they want in return? If the dude or dudette doesn't appear to be associated with any group or club, and if their answer is that they are doing it for nothing or that they're doing it because you seem like a nice person who seems lost and they want to help you out, be very cautious.

2. Do they have verifiable experience? Do any of your friends know them? Can you get a reference? Do they have any sort of reputation to support their offer?

3. Do they straight away suggest that you go somewhere private with them?

4. Does all their equipment look conspicuously new? This may indicate that so are they.

5. Do they encourage you to get out and talk to people? If they try to hide you away or "protect" you from others who might give you the wrong idea, beware! They may be trying to keep you ignorant and thus be better able to manipulate you.

# 7.11   The gift of submission

One of the ideas which seems to have gained a footing in some sections of this very large BDSM community of which we are a part is the "gift of submission".

I can understand where the idea comes from. Many submissives have intense feelings of vulnerability in their first BDSM experiences. They feel like they have been opened up, that their protective barriers have been peeled away, and that their innermost selves have been revealed. They feel completely exposed to their dominant. This is very powerful, very personal, and very intimate. These submissives perhaps feel more naked than they ever have in the past. It's special. It can be so new and amazing that they can't imagine anyone else ever feeling the same.

And because they feel that this rarely or never-before exposed inner part of themselves is being presented to their partner they may see it as a special gift from them to their partner, that this usually-protected, delicate, and valuable part of themselves is

*Wrong reasons why people do BDSM*

being opened up for their partner to see and explore. In a sense, it truly is a gift.

But funnily enough, their dominant partner may be going through much the same thing, through the same intensity and the same emotional roller-coaster. Their dominant may be feeling hungers, urges, and drives which are new to them too. They can experience a need to open themselves up, to reveal, and to explore these feelings with their submissive partner. It is the same, but from the other side. The idea of a "gift of dominance" though, doesn't seem to get anywhere near the same amount of traction as the idea of a "gift of submission".

The idea that any of this is a gift from one person to the other, regardless of which direction we're talking about, is misleading and can be manipulative. In most relationships—certainly in balanced and healthy ones—what each partner gives and gets should be in equally satisfying proportions. Indeed, this is probably what you should be striving for all the time with your partner. But if you convince your partner that you are giving them this amazing "gift" then you have created a bargaining position for yourself where you can demand things from them in return: "I have given you my gift of submission and now you need to do all these things for me because my gift is so amazingly and obviously valuable that you'll have to work hard to really earn and keep it."

Sometimes this unfortunate attitude rises to a greater height when the person afflicted by this view promotes the gift to a treasure and, in fact, they themselves become the treasure. I confess that I call my partner "treasure" sometimes. I also call her "snookums" and a few other cute names. I do however hold firmly with the belief that neither of us is gold-plated. We're both human, and we give and take in this relationship in accordance with our abilities.

Your partner is valuable to you because they allow you to experience this gift. Rather than being a gift which you give to your partner, it is a gift which your partner allows you to give yourself. Whether you are a dominant or a submissive, top or bottom, your partner is the one who works with you to create a context or environment where your own powerful inner feelings can surface and be explored in safety.

The truth is, I think, that there are no diamond-studded gifts of submission. You're there because the feelings your partner is helping you experience are rewarding, intense, and even amazing for you. Show your gratitude for their time and for their efforts, and help them get the same sort of amazing feelings themselves.

If you're a dominant and you encounter a submissive or bottom who earnestly tries to sell you the idea of a "gift of submission", I suggest that you say you're not buying and straight away start looking for someone who will be there to share with you.

# 7.12   Let me serve you

I think service can be great. It's a sign that the person giving it is prepared to let my wants and needs influence or control their choices and actions. It's a sign that satisfying me is important to them. It doesn't need to be anything big, such as painting my house, or anything intimate, such as sex. It can be something simple, like rubbing my shoulders or bringing me a drink. Even little things, like a friend buying me some popcorn at the cinema at the same time they're buying theirs can be very pleasant.

*Wrong reasons why people do BDSM*

In BDSM, service can be an excellent exercise in power. A service-oriented submissive or dominant takes their cues from their partner whose needs they want to satisfy. The service-oriented person responds to these and generally enjoys the feedback or signs of appreciation they get from their partner for a job well done.

This sometimes doesn't work quite as constructively as you might hope.

## "Let me serve you"

Over the years, one of the phrases which I have become increasingly cautious about hearing from a submissive is something which sounds like, "Let me serve you." The reason I am cautious is that it's frequently an invitation for me to do a lot of work with little in return.

The clues that this is the case are:

1. The submissive concerned has a list of things I'm allowed to ask them to do. They may not actually phrase it like that. Instead, they might be more subtle and have "limits" which prevent me doing anything except what they want,

2. The things I can ask them to do are heavy on personal reward or convenience for them and light on what I get out of it. For example, I may ask them to bring me a sandwich at a play party, and they may do this with much chatting with others and dilly-dallying along the way to the extent that I have to wait half an hour for my food. I, however, must still be grateful and tell them what a good girl they are because they brought me a sandwich,

3. I'm required to be an active participant before, during, and after these activities, and

4. None of the things they'll be doing actually require any particular skill, talent, or effort.

The submissives who do this are sometimes called "do me" submissives. They are looking for a partner to give them all the thrills they want without offering anything substantial in return. What you hear from them can sound like this:

> *"If you adopt a stern voice and let me bow my head to you, I will get you a can of soft drink from the refrigerator in the corner. You must also show your appreciation once I hand the drink to you by patting me on the head, telling me what a good girl I am, and for the rest of the evening telling everyone else what a good girl I am because I got you a can of drink from the refrigerator."*

Of course, if this is all there is to it then—as in the case of the abovementioned sandwich—I'm far better off getting the can of soft drink for myself.

You might also hear:

> *"I will let you lead me around on a leash for the evening."*

And this benefits me how?

Or:

> *"I will serve you by allowing you to tie me up any way I want."*

*Wrong reasons why people do BDSM*

Again, if I can only tie her up how she wants, how does this benefit me?

And finally:

> *"I will serve you by sucking your cock as long as I feel like it."*

I don't know about you, but if you—the reader—are equipped with a cock and are like me, then having it sucked is quite nice. But I am actually looking for more than that. There seem to be many submissives who go—pardon the expression—into their own small little world while sucking cock and are actually largely uninterested in the cock owner's enjoyment.

A good way to work out what's happening when someone insists that they are truly interested only in serving you is to mention a book such as *Butlers & Household Managers: 21st Century Professionals*[4]. It is about providing excellent personal service, and it's a very good book which I strongly recommend. It is, however, quite amazing how many submissives who say they're keen to serve you have absolutely no interest in reading it. At first glance, this might be surprising because someone who swears they absolutely exist only to serve would presumably want to do a good job and any tips or clues on how to serve better would clearly be extremely valuable. Of course, their lack of enthusiasm tells you straight away that they're not interested in serving you well at all. They're actually interested in serving themselves.

The point is that they're looking to get you to make an effort to provide a context where they can get their jollies. Some

---

[4] [FERRY2008]

submissives and slaves, for example, get off far more on being told what to do than on actually doing it. For others, the tasks must be simple, easy, and unchallenging, and they expect great praise, pats on the head, and compliments from you in return.

It is perhaps not dissimilar to insisting that you should be grateful that they've bared their back so you can flog it, or that you hallow their name because they've spread their legs so you can fuck them because, quite clearly, this is such amazing service to you and they, of course, get absolutely nothing out of it and it is complete self-sacrifice on their part. See also above where I talked about *The gift of submission* (p. 56).

The things to look for here are the submissives who:

- Are keen for you to know what you can do for them and the things they love to experience,

- Don't think to tell you what they can do for you, and

- Seem to care remarkably little for what you actually want or need and will change the subject if you try to tell them.


Now. I'm not trying to tar all submissives with the same brush. Far be it. But the point of this chapter is to stress that there are some submissives who consciously or unconsciously will be looking strictly at what you can do for them, rather than what they can also do for you. In some cases I am sure it is simply ignorance, that they just can't comprehend that more than a token effort from them is required for it actually to be meaningful and useful service.

*Wrong reasons why people do BDSM*

## Questions and discussion

Healthy BDSM relationships are about wants and needs being met on both sides. Because the ways of BDSM can be subtle, the wants and needs involved in even a healthy relationship can be challenging to identify.

If you're feeling uneasy about your relationship with your partner, or if you don't know whether you are satisfying their needs, or if you don't think yours are being addressed, it can be worthwhile to sit down with them and ask:

- In each of the activities you do with your partner:

    - Which of your needs are you attempting to satisfy?
    - How successful is this activity at achieving that?
    - Which of your partner's needs are you attempting to satisfy?
    - How successful is the activity at achieving this?

- Are there any of your wants or needs which don't seem to be being addressed at all?

- Are there any of your partner's wants or needs which don't seem to be being addressed?

- Do you feel you are doing much more than your partner?

- Does your partner feel they are doing much more of the work than you?

# 7.13   Recognising the pretenders

A lot of what I've been writing about in this chapter has to do with pretenders. A pretender is faking some or all of their interest so you'll willingly or unwillingly help them satisfy their need. They may be looking to you simply as someone to fuck, to hurt, or to help build up their ego. It's selfish and it's all about them. Because of this, and in the worst cases:

- They don't want you to find out the truth. They'll have barriers up around themselves and won't let you in more than superficially. You'll likely feel the distance between them and you, and they won't do anything to help you get closer to them.

- They aren't really interested in your needs *per se*, and instead are only interested in what they must do to get you to comply with their needs. In particular, they won't be interested in you reciprocating their faked interest in BDSM. For example, if they discover that tying you up makes you horny and sexually receptive then they may claim to be a great bondage enthusiast. However, if you offer yourself to be tied up where sex isn't a possibility—such as a quick tie in an empty subway car between stops—they'll never be interested.

- If they're looking to hurt you then they may tend to avoid warm ups and go straight for heavy or intense play. They may justify this by coming up with an excuse that it's for your benefit, training or education.

- The shortest distance between two points is a straight line and if sex is their game then they'll only be interested in

*Wrong reasons why people do BDSM*

the straightest line to your cunt or to your cock. They'll demonstrate a consistent lack of enthusiasm for exploring anything else or spending more time than necessary to get between your legs.

## 7.14   Conclusion

I've talked about it before and it merits mention again. Maturity, self-awareness, and responsibility are important in making relationships work, and BDSM ones especially. When the stakes are low and only fluffy pink handcuffs are involved then perhaps not so much. But as the stakes increase—for you or for your partner—the need for personal maturity increases along with them.

A big part of maturity, self-awareness, and responsibility is being open with yourself and with your partner. The things which make many of the reasons for getting involved in BDSM mentioned in this chapter into bad reasons are the selfishness, dishonesty, and lack of openness associated with them.   In BDSM terms, there's nothing wrong with wanting to flog your partner until blood runs down their back, or to tie them and fuck them until their cunt is raw. For it to be positive and rewarding for you both, it does need to be something that you're open and passionate about, not something hidden.

# Chapter 8

# Recognising pitfalls and obstacles

Like any other relationships between two people, BDSM relationships can and do fail. There are traps we can fall into which can lead to temporary or complete breakdowns of our relationships. While this is true for all relationships, BDSM has traps and pitfalls which are unique. They occur in no other types of relationships.

One of the big problems with trying to have a successful BDSM relationship is that because of the underground nature of BDSM we don't grow up surrounded by prototypes of good, healthy, well-functioning, BDSM relationships as vanilla folk do. We lack a regular exposure to examples of how things should or shouldn't be done BDSM-wise. BDSM tends to be hidden, and while vanilla folk constantly get to see vanilla-type relationships play out amongst family, friends, in the media, and in movies, we BDSM folk are often in the situation of having to make it up as we go along. This causes us to be particularly susceptible to some types of mistakes:

- Mistakes made out of ignorance,

- Placing obstacles in our own way, or in the way of our partner,

- The mistake of confusing others' outrageous fantasies—as portrayed in movies, books, or porn—with reality. These mistakes are particularly prevalent at the beginning of our journey,

- Being easily conned or mislead, and

- Falling for predators.

In this chapter I'll be looking at some of these mistaken ideas, at some predators who knowingly or unknowingly take advantage of this naïveté, and at some of the unique ways a BDSM relationship can fail.

# 8.1   Been there. Done that

Many aspects of BDSM can be interesting and exciting because:

- They can involve nude members of the opposite sex, or

- They are new and unusual.

In my neck of the woods, nude members of the opposite sex tend to be regarded as a good thing, but even full-frontal nudity can pale after a while, and nudity on its own is not BDSM anyway.

Also, the world of BDSM is quite large and it can take a lot of exploration to exhaust all of the possibilities. Initially, it can seem like there's always something new and unusual to try because there are so many different ways of practising BDSM. Unfortunately, there does come a time when you've tried all the different BDSM implements, positions, and styles. If your main motivator was the novelty and now the novelty is gone, what next?

This is an important question because some people get into BDSM precisely because it's new, risky, confronting, illicit, unusual, shocking, and perhaps even just because it seems like a kinky way to spice up sex. If the BDSM is not satisfying in itself, or if the BDSM is worth doing merely because you've never done this sort of thing before, then the time when it doesn't excite any more is already on the horizon.

It can take a fair while to get to this point. Maybe months, possibly years, particularly if the BDSM brings other benefits such as a sexy partner.

It can sometimes be obvious when the novelty is a significant factor. If you or your partner are often driven to look for new BDSM activities, new places to do your BDSM, new fetish clothes, new BDSM toys, and new people to do it with, then maybe you should reflect on exactly what you want out of BDSM with your partner. There's absolutely nothing wrong with exploration, but if the only thing you have is the exploration then your BDSM may be in trouble.

## 8.2   When you don't know the real you

For BDSM to be satisfying and rewarding it needs to match up with your own wants and, importantly, needs. This is, I hope, obvious. Yet for reasons of guilt, fear, social pressure, or ego, many people twist what they do in the dungeon away from what they need and towards what they <u>think</u> they should be doing. This may not be something they do consciously; it can be due to ways of thinking they've unconsciously learned in the past. This means that instead of the right BDSM for them, they instead end up doing nearly-right BDSM or even the wrong BDSM.

Ego can be a big factor here. The voice in the back of your mind which, each time you look in the mirror, tells you that the face you see could be a movie star, is the same one which might say in the dungeon:

- "I am the most sexually desirable person in this dungeon and the guys/ladies should be falling over themselves to spend time with me!"

- "My sexual prowess has no equal and 'huge dick' is a clear understatement!"

- "I am the most dominant master in the room and I can dominate anyone or anything at any time! I can also fix anything mechanical, I fully understand abstract physics, have discovered two new planets with only a pair of binoculars, have created a cure for politics, and I construct working nuclear reactors in my spare time using only paper clips!"

- "My submission is a thing of art and beauty which none can rival!"

*Recognising pitfalls and obstacles*

Fear of being seen—by yourself or by others—as being merely mortal may be a part of this. In addition, by thinking of yourself as a clearly superior specimen it means that if you don't get laid or don't get a date on Saturday night that you can blame others for their short-sightedness rather than deal with the fact that you're not such a great catch after all. My experience is that guys are particularly affected, but women aren't far behind in their own way. With guys it is often dick-related, even if just figuratively. With women, well... they also sometimes feel the need to compete for a partner. The point is that many people into BDSM have something to prove, and for this reason they are often not presenting themselves as they truly and deeply are. They consciously or unconsciously try to present themselves as shiny and flawless, and this even extends to the activities they engage in with their partner.

Regardless of where it comes from, it means that these folk aren't getting what they need out of BDSM. Instead they're getting what they'd like to think they need. A guy who actually has a strong submissive streak but who feels compelled to "act the dom" is certainly going to miss out. Likewise, a woman who has been taught that her place is at the feet of a strong man is not going to be able to comfortably pick up a flogger and attend to her partner even though it might really be the right thing for both of them.

It's worth reflecting a while on what factors contribute to how you define yourself. If you see yourself as a dominant, why is that? Is ego a part of this choice? Do you feel a need to avoid signs of weakness? How do you feel about a woman being in control? Or what about a man being in control? Do you feel guilty about what you do? How do you feel about hitting your partner? Is there some standard you're trying to achieve? Who set this standard?

If you call yourself a submissive, what is it about you that makes you think that? Is it the things you like doing? If it's just what you get out of the physical side of BDSM, what about the mental side? Does part of you shy away from taking control even though it's something you often think about? When you do kneel, how does it feel? Is there something in you which makes you think that kneeling is bad? Do you feel guilty about it?

## 8.3   Trying too fiercely to be independent

Following on from the above, one of the things we learn in our western society is to be independent and to do things for ourselves. Frequently this is not the right thing to do in BDSM, particularly for dominants. This is because many submissives like doing things for their dominant partner. They like to serve. For some, it is a need to serve. It is part of their submissive experience and it is satisfying and rewarding for them. In serving they submit to the commands, to the wants, or to the needs of their dominant.

When a dominant tries to do everything for himself he can be preventing his submissive partner from actually being submissive. He takes away from him or her the chance to submit. More than that, at the same time he also takes away his own chance to take charge, to take control, to dominate his submissive partner, and so he misses out as well.

There isn't anything wrong with being independent and doing things yourself if there are good reasons. But being a dominant means you have a duty to dominate, otherwise you should take down your shingle and go and find some other role.   And dominating means directing and taking charge. It means having your submissive do what you want. It's part of the deal you have with them. Token tasks are not enough. You need them to be doing useful and meaningful things for you. This doesn't need to be all the time, but it needs to be enough of the time.

You're not sacrificing your independence by having your submissive do things for you. You are merely choosing not to assert it. Sure, you could go and get your own coffee, but if you send your submissive then you both get some pleasure—you by being dominant, and she by serving.

A dominant may inappropriately assert their independence for many reasons:

- Personal insecurity,

- His or her ego,

- Their self-image,

- Some form of denial or guilt to the extent that he feels he can't allow his partner to keep doing things for him, or

- As a symbolic way of avoiding commitment by insisting on doing things for him- or herself.

**Personal insecurity** can come from self-doubt, from not being sure that he can adopt the appropriate air of authority, or from not being sure how his submissive is actually going to take being told what to do. This latter may be valid because some submissives will only submit to rope or the lash, and trying to tell them what to do away from rope and floggers may get you the finger.

Communication is a big help with personal insecurity. If you're the dominant and you're not sure, ask. It's the dominant thing to do. If you're the submissive and you have a strong desire or need to serve, then say so and be openly and obviously receptive to direction and command. Encourage your dominant to take charge of you through your attitude and responses.

**Ego** can appear in thoughts such as: "I am the great MegaSupaWundaDom[1]! I am powerful! I am supreme!" When this happens any sign of dependence on another—such as a submissive doing something useful for MSWD—can't be tolerated because it damages the super-ness of his or her image. Any submissive in the picture just gets to do menial and insignificant tasks which don't impact the dominant in any way. MSWD won't allow the submissive to be particularly effective and while MSWD will happily use and take advantage of their submissive, they won't allow the submissive to dent their armour or penetrate them in any way. It is entirely one way. For some submissives this can be appealing for a while, but BDSM is about the dominant and the submissive affecting each other, about the submissive being empowered and enabled to be submissive by their partner, and by the dominant being empowered and able to exercise their dominance by their submissive. MSWD won't allow the latter and tries to be self-empowering. Ultimately, this sort of behaviour is about fear, and it is self-defeating and hollow.

While ego often relates to a more-than-perfect image of oneself, there are other forms of **self-image** which can interfere with a BDSM relationship. When the self-image is a false one, i.e., it does not accurately reflect the inner person, then it must get in the way of a satisfying BDSM relationship. The reason it must get in the way is that when we have a false self-image we work

---

[1] Also known as MSWD.

to satisfy the needs we think this false self-image has rather than our own real needs. Likewise, our partner relates to this same self-image we project rather than the real us and this reduces how much we can feel engaged by them.

Thinking that you can't be a dominant because a) striking or tying up your partner is not a right or honourable thing to do, and b) you're not like that, is possibly a throwback to your upbringing. Many dominants have this particular burdensome image which limits what they do.

In a similar way, a person with strong submissive wants or needs may be prevented from fully exploring them because of an image of themselves as an individual who kneels to no one.

**Denial or guilt** can prevent a dominant taking full advantage of his enthusiastic submissive. Feelings of inferiority can be the basis here. Rather than fully appreciating the attention and obedience of his submissive, a dominant suffering from guilt, inferiority, or one who is in some form of denial, will have feelings that he should be doing things for his submissive rather than, correctly, the other way around. In fact, by having his submissive attend him and serve him he may be doing the very best for her. This may even seem paradoxical to him.

Finally, and ominously, a dominant who was otherwise fine, may start becoming independent as an unconscious sign that he or she is getting cold feet and is starting to push their submissive away. This can be a **fear of commitment** rearing its head. He might argue that it's because of the joy or satisfaction he gets from getting his own hands dirty, or because he likes things done "his way", but you need to be cautious here. Such an argument might be an entirely valid reason for him to do some things himself, but not everything. And certainly not if his submissive could do the things equally well. On the other hand, arguing that he enjoys getting his hands dirty may be an excuse rather than a reason, an excuse which he might be making entirely unconsciously. It can be like a vanilla guy spending too much time tinkering with his car in the garage instead of being with his wife. The car and the tinkering becomes an excuse to avoid the wife.

When a submissive complains that his or her dominant won't let her do things for him, or that she's never given any serious tasks or duties, any of the reasons above can be the cause. In all of the above situations, communication with your partner, introspection, and, above all, honesty with yourself are the keys to resolving them.

## 8.4   Failing to transition from training to use

When a dominant and a submissive or a master and a slave set up shop together, one of the things which the dominant or master may do is begin to train the submissive or slave. This can be a mutually satisfying and exciting time in the relationship.

For some BDSM partnerships, the training can take the form of the dominant or master teaching his new partner about the various activities he does. This can be the way he conducts an impact play scene, how he runs a pain play scene, the positions, postures and implements he prefers to use, and so on. For a dominant with a service-oriented submissive or slave the training might also consist of assigning duties, monitoring how well they are performed, applying correction, etc. In either case, the dominant has a lot to communicate to his partner, and this can be a very "hands on" and rewarding process.

What happens when the training phase is over? When the submissive or slave is educated in the ways of the master, or when the submissive has learned all the tasks and duties her partner desires her to do, what then?

The risk—and, indeed, the consequence—for many is summed up in the typical Internet post shown in figure 8.1 on the following page.

Training can't go on forever. At some point, the person who is being trained has learned all their trainer or partner has to offer. After training, what comes next?

The ideal answer is use. Once a submissive or slave has been sufficiently trained, the dominant should be able to use the submissive according to how she has been trained. If she's a service-oriented submissive, then she should be serving him drinks, cooking his food, performing oral sex on him, etc. If she's been trained instead to absorb all the punishment he can hand out in the dungeon, then that's where she should shine and he be happiest. We've seen though that one of the key parts of BDSM is penetration. During training of a slave or submissive, there is a lot of penetration between the master and the submissive. The master is constantly monitoring or correcting. Once the training is over, the level of penetration often drops dramatically. Certainly, the slave or submissive will be useful in their own way, but the dominant doesn't really get to be dominant to the same extent as during training, and the slave may well feel left alone or even abandoned because while their partner is still there physically, the actual D&s penetration has gone.

We can see this happening in the example in the Internet post. The initial phase of this slave's relationship with her master was based on training. This required her master to compel or

Dear mailing list,

When my master and I first began our relationship he knew exactly what he wanted and expected from me. I put in a *lot* of time, effort and struggle to adjust so that I could be the slave he wanted me to be.

I remember how hard it was. Many of my most personal beliefs and values were challenged by all this—not just because he was asking for a lot, but also because I had to confront myself and really closely examine what it was that I wanted and needed. The exchange of power which I felt with each way of thinking I confronted, and with each behaviour I learned or unlearned was palpable.

Now most of the challenges from the early days are behind me. I have adapted so that all his requirements and expectations are second nature to me now.

But now I have a question: because all the change in me has been done, does this mean that there is no more power exchange between us?

Slave Sue

Figure 8.1: Failed training-to-use transition post

*Recognising pitfalls and obstacles*

require her to achieve standards which he set. The intensity of the penetration she felt came from his determination. As she says, "he knew exactly what he wanted and expected".

But once she has learned how to behave or not behave, and has learned the standards and values which her master requires, the penetration stops happening. There is no need for any effort from him to reshape her. Indeed, there is no need for her to reshape herself in light of his needs or desires because she has already done so.

This is a common scenario when any form of training is involved. At some point, the trainer has done all of the training possible. What then? In the case of someone who is purely a trainer, the trainee (the slave in this case) goes back to their owner to be used.

However, in the example we have a trainer who is also nominally the master or owner of this slave, but the transition from trainer to owner hasn't occurred. What appears to have happened is that there has been an awkward fading from trainer-who-trains to trainer-who-doesn't-have-anything-to-train, and this is, of course, unsatisfactory (probably for both concerned).

There's a big difference between how a trainer engages their trainee and how an owner or master engages their slave. The risk with failing to make this transition properly is that you end up with something like the above example—namely someone who is in service but who is not being engaged or penetrated.

The main problem is that new BDSM couples faced with this often started out in their relationship recognising that training would be very exciting and powerful for them both. In fact, it can be intensely exciting, and it is one of the main, easy ways of getting a lot of engagement and interaction with lots of expressions of power. Wonderful!

However, phase two is often neglected. What do you do with a trained slave or submissive that will engage both you and them? If your slave is trained to serve coffee with immaculate perfection, then while the training phase might have been intense and painful, once trained the slave doesn't need correction and, in fact, possibly won't need any correction or masterly expressions from their partner ever again. And, of course, serving then becomes a chore or unsatisfying because it's no longer about a productive BDSM engagement and exploring and experiencing power, it's merely about coffee.

There are a couple of ways around this problem.

Pessimistically, you could simply accept that there won't be any joy once training is complete. You simply move on to a new partner. In fact, this happens rather a lot.

Alternatively, you could plan for the use phase well before the training ends (preferably even before you set yourself up with your trainee). Having concrete goals for your trained submissive which include opportunities for you to command and direct them, to engage them, and to create situations where they can feel used and even objectified, may keep the relationship ticking along quite nicely.

- You could use your submissive as a tool in activities you usually perform just by yourself. For example, if you do your own car maintenance, or run your own business, or do your own computer repairs, then while you are busy with this use your submissive to fetch things, to watch a screen, to hold something, etc. If you enjoy cooking, put them to work cutting onions or celery, or stirring the pots while you do more critical things like adding spices or cooking the meat.

- Try to avoid "invisible service". This is where your submissive or slave does things so that you aren't involved at all. While this may be OK for a servant you employ, it can be a disaster in D&s. Instead, make sure you are involved authoritatively in most or all of the service they perform, such as your approval being required for the breakfast, lunch, and dinner menus each and every day before they are prepared; your submissive not being allowed to dress in the morning until you have chosen or approved their clothes; them not being allowed to arrange outside activities—such as shopping, hairdresser appointments, social visits, pleasure outings, etc.—without your prior approval in each case.

Unfortunately, some people can't make this transition from training to use. A lot of the time, in fact, it's probably and actually inappropriate because it is the training itself which is what is exciting for the master and for the slave.

We live in a society where we are encouraged to do for ourselves and this makes using someone (as opposed to training someone) a difficult step for many. I have come across a number of masters who are quite comfortable with the training, or the tying up, or the flogging of their partners, but who are very uncomfortable with being served. Instead of preparing the daily chores, or assigning tasks or errands to their slave partners, they do the things themselves.

Tasks, duties and errands also provide opportunities for penetration and engagement. A master need not make this up just to keep their partner busy, but can take their own ordinary, everyday activities and farm them out to their slave. For example, sending one's slave out to do the banking, chase up quotes for a job, organise invitations to party, or get master's car repaired, can all provide exciting and satisfying duties for a service-oriented slave.

Once training is done—and if he successfully makes the transition from trainer to master—the master then gets to direct her in the execution of the tasks and duties he assigns her. In return he, ideally, gets to see his projects being developed and pushed forward by more than just him. Done well, he will feel that his slave is an extension of his will and desire which is focussed on his personal priorities. His slave will feel herself being moved and directed by his determination.

A final note here: once training is completed, the master must also have goals which he expects and wants to use his slave to achieve, such as to have her perform as *maître d'* at his formal dinner parties, or to help him run his business. Her uniqueness then determines how these goals are achieved. This is important because rather than the goals being achieved as he would do them himself, she achieves the goals with her own unique stamp. When the service slave is combined with a master, the end result is not merely the same work as the master would do multiplied by two, but is instead the master's goals and projects achieved by two unique individuals working towards them.

# 8.5   Power decay

Failing to transition from training to use is an example of what we could call power decay. One of the pillars of BDSM and of BDSM relationships is a disparity of power, and one of the main sources of power in BDSM is motivation or drive. When a dominant has a strong drive to tie up, hurt, flog, or control their partner then this is a power that they have. This is an intensity which they can express with their partner.

While a top or dominant may have a significantly higher skill level at some BDSM activities than their submissive, or they may be physically stronger than their submissive, often it is the need or desire to use this skill or strength which is the actual source of power which the dominant feels and which their submissive is subject to.

When hunger, drive, or passion diminishes, power tends to diminish with them. Failing to transition from training to use may simply mean that the dominant or master concerned has a strong drive or need to train his submissive, but that he then doesn't have a strong need to use her once she is trained. When this is the case, his passion or drive is obviously going to diminish as her training with him reaches its end. The disparity of power component of their BDSM fades, and with it goes any penetration both he or she may feel.

This decay in power can occur for other reasons. For example:

- When BDSM is used to satisfy a need, a change in circumstances may mean that the need disappears. Someone with a stressful job who used BDSM for catharsis may not need it any more if they change to a less stressful job.

- A submissive who enters into BDSM looking simply for pain or hotter-sex-through-bondage may find that as their tastes become more refined and as they gain experience that simple rope play or a quick flogging no longer does it for them. Their current partner may not be able to go where they need to go and so the submissive effectively disempowers their dominant as they outgrow them.

- BDSM may initially seem exciting or titillating, and this novelty may be enough to maintain the passion, but with experience the novelty will necessarily fade and if it was the novelty which was keeping the fires alive then the power fades with it.

# 8.6 Imagination, images and engagement

One of the issues I see which causes a breakdown in BDSM relationships is actually more of a failure to start them properly. This is related to something I explored in *This Curious Human Phenomenon*[2], namely how is it possible for two people to meet at a BDSM play party, chat for a while, and then go off into a convenient dungeon and have a most intense BDSM scene? How can a dominant engage and penetrate so intensely someone he or she has only just met? How can a submissive have such an intimate experience with someone she doesn't really know?

I wrote in *Curious* that they weren't actually having such an intense experience with the actual person, but instead were largely projecting their own internal ideas and needs onto this person they had just met. In their own minds, they imagine that this person they have just met is more than they actually are. They project an image of their ideal partner onto this new person, even if they aren't an ideal fit.

This is OK strictly in this play party context because it serves to get things started and let off some steam. But it's only

---

[2][MASTERS2008, pp. 77 - 87]

useful in this play party context. Beyond the play party the whole experience can be misleading because it might suggest that there's some actual chemistry involved.

Let's look at this a little more.

Suppose a guy goes to a party and meets an amazing vision of female goddess-ness. If she deigns to speak to him or, amazingly, rests her feet on him or gets him to fetch her a drink, then he might have a most powerful reaction. But who or what is he really reacting to? If he has just met her then it can't be her. She might have just walked in the door and he feels compelled to drop to his knees. But it can't be her who he is reacting to because he doesn't know her at all. He may later discover that she, in fact, is not dominant in any way but that doesn't stop him getting turned on in this first instant.

If he can't be reacting to her, then he must be reacting to an image in his own mind of how a female dominant should look or act. This process frequently happens when one person sees or meets another, and it may work to kick start a relationship—i.e., "I'll spend time with you because you look like the sort of person I'd like to spend time with".

However, for a relationship starting this way to go the distance, a transformation needs to occur. Instead of being excited by the image in our mind of our partner, we need to become excited by this partner themselves. For the abovementioned guy and the female dominant, he needs to be excited by her herself rather than by the image in his mind which excited him initially.

Trying to continue a relationship just with an image is like masturbation. It's having a relationship with yourself. While this may be nice—and certainly precludes disappointment—there is little engagement with your actual partner and hence it's not going to lead to a satisfying BDSM relationship.

Some BDSM activities are more likely candidates in which such image relationships can occur or persist than others. Flogging is a good example. The most common targets for flogging are the back or buttocks. Due to the way we humans are built, most floggings are not done face-to-face. This means that during flogging neither the dominant nor the submissive gets to see their partner's facial expressions, winces, grunts, or exertions. This is ideal territory for relating to an image rather than our real partner because if we can't see our partner's face, how can we really engage or connect with them?

Indeed, most of the time we might not be connecting with them at all during a flogging scene but instead be connecting to an image of them. Because we can't see their face, we might be imagining or guessing how they feel or how they are responding. We might base this on what we know about them in particular, or on our previous experience with other partners.

When we can't directly communicate with our partner, such as when we can't see their face, or when they are covered up during mummification or are wearing a hood, we rely on other signals and messages. These other messages and signals which we get from our partner and which help us to engage them, especially when we can't see their faces, include hand-waving, grunts, moans, wiggles, writhes, muscle movements, laughs, and even occasional words or phrases. But even with these we might interpret a particular wriggle as meaning one thing when our partner is really feeling something else.

This is where engagement with our real partner comes in. As we learn about our partner and become familiar with their actions and reactions, we have less of a need to fill in the gaps with our imagination or from how previous partners reacted because we know our partner and don't need to guess or imagine. Getting back to flogging as an example, this means that when they wriggle a certain way or make a particular sound we don't have to guess what this means or try to think back to how other submissives or dominants behaved. We know exactly what it means, and thus we are engaging our real partner rather than an image in our mind or some generic or average partner from our past experience.

This leads us to one of the problems with some BDSM scenes: it can be hard to feel engagement with your partner when they are playing at being a dead fish (i.e., not moving or responding in an obvious way but hopefully not really dead). This feedback is vitally important both to preventing the image problem, and to allowing our partners to feel engaged and penetrated by us.

Being able to engage our real and actual partners means knowing what they feel, how they react, and what they mean when they communicate with us. After a scene we tune into this more by sitting down with them and talking about how they feel, what they were thinking during the scene, what certain actions or sounds meant and so on. At the same time, we share our thoughts and reactions with them so they can be better tuned in to us.

# 8.7   Testing and challenges

A submissive or slave who needs to feel a firm hand—metaphorically speaking—is going to tug on their metaphoric leash from time to time to check that their partner is still paying attention. They do this when they feel that perhaps they have too much freedom, or that their partner isn't supervising or correcting them sufficiently.

Remember that BDSM is about penetration and if a slave or submissive isn't feeling sufficiently penetrated by their partner then they may consciously or unconsciously do things to get a reaction from their partner. They may become disrespectful, inattentive, or downright disobedient.

There are, of course, SAMs (Smart-Assed Masochists) who may deliberately be disrespectful, frisky, or mischievous to provoke a reaction from their partner, often as a power play (i.e., to try to demonstrate that they're in charge). But others may be doing it because they are genuinely feeling a lack of something from their partner.

If you notice that your submissive or slave partner has periods of restlessness, lack of attention, or disobedience, then look to see if it is their way of getting you to tighten things up. They may be feeling a lack of direction from you, and just a little more attention from you in regards to their discipline may be all that they require.

## Sabotage

A SAM may also behave the way they do defensively. When they are consciously or unconsciously afraid they can behave in a smart-assed way to change the course of what's going on to protect themselves. For example, if they are unconsciously afraid of the intensity of their feelings once these feelings are released, or are afraid of surrendering to their own reactions with someone they don't know well or who they don't trust, they may do something to irritate or annoy that person or to deflect what they're doing so as to reduce the threat of exposing themselves or of becoming too vulnerable. It can be the case that they don't consciously know why they do this. As they say, "I don't know why I did that."

What they're doing is sabotage to prevent themselves getting into a situation which scares them. For example, a submissive who knows that they easily slip into a state of surrender or sub-space in which they are quite vulnerable might still enjoy the attentions of a dominant, but when the action or context starts to get close to where she might get triggered, she'll do something to deflect this, to change the context to one where she feels safe again. Being a smart ass is one way of doing this.

In section 8.15 on page 106 we'll see some other strategies which are specifically aimed at avoiding surrender.

## 8.8   Boredom

If BDSM stops inspiring you or your partner for some reason it can manifest itself in a few obvious ways:

- Boredom with what you and your partner are doing together,

- Feeling that what used to be satisfying is now merely ho-hum,

- The difficulty and challenge is gone. What used to be demanding and hard work is now such familiar territory that you can do it with your eyes closed and one hand tied behind your back (which may actually be the case anyway!), or

- Not feeling a connection with your partner any more. You're both going through the motions, and the BDSM activities themselves still work mechanically, but it's like there's no one on the other end of the flogger.

It might be that the original reasons you and your partner got into BDSM are no longer there. Some people outgrow BDSM. For others, their life circumstances change and BDSM loses the importance it once had. If you feel that your BDSM has lost its edge, talk with your partner. Maybe exploring some other areas of BDSM will bring the zing back.

## 8.9   Failure to communicate

Many relationship problems come down to poor communication. Talk deeply and talk often. Don't let things get bad before saying something. Don't feel embarrassed. Be open. Don't judge.

The important thing about all this is that some BDSM misconceptions can get in the way of communication. I've mentioned a few already in this series of books, but communication is always a topic worth revisiting.

Although a dominant is supposed to be in charge, they aren't necessarily supposed to have all the answers. That doesn't mean that your submissive will either, but they are another source of information. When you don't know what to do or are puzzled then ask. Admitting that you don't know is more a sign of strength than weakness, and it can often indicate that you want to include your partner rather than exclude them. This is a good thing. Muddling on when there is better information available, or when your partner can help, is not a sign of strength and can seriously damage your image in the eyes of your partner and of those people around you, e.g., other BDSM folk.

If you're a submissive then the story is similar. Just because you wear a label that says "submissive" or "slave" doesn't mean that you know what to do, what to think, or how to achieve everything. If you don't know how to do something, say so. E.g., if you don't know how to do a slick 3-step kneel and how to smoothly rise to your feet, find someone to show you or who will teach you. Don't just cobble something together and hope it's right.

There's an odd idea about that you should be able to do everything yourself. Learning the physical and mental skills to be an effective submissive is not always easy, and you might not be able to learn them just on your own or just with your usual partner. Ditto for dominants. If you are married and you and your partner have only just discovered BDSM, it can be difficult to consider going outside the marriage to learn more. But learning about BDSM, getting training on how to tie knots or how to flog, getting tips and advice from other dominants and submissives, or even inviting someone along to your own private dungeon to show you both how some BDSM activities work, is not going to violate your marriage oaths.

Communicate with your partner. Communicate with other BDSM folk. Don't let ego or insecurity get in the way.

# 8.10   Not showing reactions

In most scenes or engagements with your dominant partner, they need you to react. They are not there just to hit you, they want and need to see you react to being hit. They need to see the effect of the pain. Likewise, your service-oriented partner doesn't bring you drinks and massage your feet because it turns them on to do so. They need to see and feel your reaction to it.

Don't be a black hole into which your partner pours their attention and energy and from which nothing escapes. Show your feelings. Respond. Wriggle. Squirm. Moan. Often it is the case that your reaction—whether you're a dominant or a submissive, master or slave—is going to be what makes things work best for you both.

Displaying your reactions creates a connection with your partner. They get to *feel* you rather than being in the poorer position of having to guess what you're feeling. In other words, displaying your reaction increases engagement.

One way of thinking of this is that rather than being two separate individuals doing BDSM together, you and your partner are a team, even a tightly-bound single unit. What you do together is not two individual experiences which just happen to be occurring in the same location at the same time. The most intense times for you both as partners in this relationship is when what happens between you is actually one intense experience which you share. The less you communicate—either verbally or non-verbally— the more it becomes two separate experiences. The more you communicate, the more it becomes one single experience.

It's not always the case that the times with your partner are one shared experience though. As we've seen, some folk have different needs than their partner and it can easily be that sometimes one partner is getting more out of it than the other, or that each is using what they're doing together to take them to two separate places.

## 8.11    Not knowing your partner's needs

If you or your partner don't say what you want or need, or you don't show how you're feeling, or you don't display any reactions to what they do, then they have to guess what you want or need. And they may get it wrong.

If you don't know what your partner needs at any particular time, clarify. This applies regardless of which side of the power fence you're on—dominant, submissive, master or slave. Avoid guessing or assuming. It can be tempting to try to guess or to assume because if you're trying to impress someone then you don't want to appear ignorant.

In the middle of an intense scene you may not want to disturb the mood by suddenly pulling off your partner's gag and quizzing them on the finer points of clitoral stimulation as regards them, or you may not want to disturb the mood by stopping the scene and asking what they're trying to achieve by hitting you *there*; but do file the question away to ask later because the more you and your partner know about what works, what doesn't work, and when, the better you will be able to relate to each other and make things work really, really well.

## 8.12    Failing to adapt to growth

Imagine, if you will, an architect straight out of university. His first few projects out in the real world may be small—a public toilet block, a fountain, an extension to someone's garage, a scenic footpath in a park, etc. He is, however, likely to grow out of doing these as his skill and experience increase. His career may lead him to happily designing suburban apartment blocks for the rest of his career, or to designing civil engineering projects such as highway interchanges or bridges. Or maybe he will end up working for years at a time on individual projects, such as office towers or tunnel links between islands. At some point though, he will find where he is most comfortable. Not every architect aspires to design the world's tallest building. Maybe he will find his place and settle there doing medium-sized urban design projects.

In any case, the point here is that while he may start out with small projects, he will invariably rise above them. Exactly where he will rise to is difficult to say. And even if two different architects rise to the same level of technical expertise and challenge, they may be working on entirely different types of projects—such as office buildings versus bridges.

Something similar happens in the world of BDSM. Someone might enter the world of BDSM via fluffy handcuffs or through fantasies of leather-clad ladies holding whips, but where they end up is often next to impossible to guess. What we can be fairly sure about is that they will grow. Their BDSM tastes and preferences will develop and mature. Perhaps even their tolerance for pain will increase.

How does this effect their partner? If it was a mutual decision by two BDSM "virgins" to enter into the world of BDSM in a serious way together, they may find that they grow closer together if their interests remain shared and they mature in parallel. But if they discover that their maturing interests are taking them in separate directions, or if one is content with less intense or less severe BDSM than the other, then they may find their relationship breaking down.

*Recognising pitfalls and obstacles*

Sometimes breakdown is unavoidable. I've seen numerous cases where a couple spends many happy years together, perhaps bringing up a family, and then one urges them both into an exploration of BDSM. After a short time one of them discovers that BDSM strikes a deep chord in them and they throw themselves into it with a passion, leaving their long-term partner trailing along behind.

When BDSM appears to be leading you in separate directions there are things you can do which may prolong your relationship. There are possibly even things you can do which may keep you together. The most important thing is—as it always is—communication.

If you feel that BDSM may be moving you and your partner apart, discuss it with them. Be open and honest. Be clear about what's important for you. In particular, be receptive and understanding of their wants and needs and look for options where you can both find what you need. Be prepared to step back and reconsider your own position.

- If your partner is interested in doing or trying things which don't motivate you at all, or which actually turn you off, look for alternatives. Look for what's behind their interests or needs. Find out if there are other things which work for you both. BDSM is a big wide world involving many, many different activities and types of relationships. Maybe something you haven't yet thought of will provide the level of satisfaction which you and your partner are seeking. In book two of this series I have a chapter called *The lists* where I categorise over two hundred different BDSM activities. Maybe you will find something there.

- Consider alternate ways of getting wants or needs met. If your partner, for example, discovers a powerful and overwhelming need for very heavy flogging and it's something you simply can't do but otherwise your relationship is sound, then maybe your partner could offer themselves up as a practice dummy for flogging training courses, or maybe you could both frequent BDSM clubs or social events where he could get his flogging needs met by someone else. You both could even consider engaging a professional BDSM mistress or master from time to time.

- Seriously look at yourself and your views on things. If your partner discovers an intense desire to be submissive and your conservative upbringing shies away from being part of this, then step back. Maybe having someone to grovel at your feet, worship the ground you walk on, give you great massages while dressed in a G-string, and bring you food and drink, are things you could learn to love and even lust after yourself.

While not always possible, if there is a solution to growing apart due to BDSM, it definitely involves communication, openness, honesty, being receptive, and being prepared to reconsider or change your position.

# 8.13 Accelerated growth

While changes in people which might affect their relationships often take a long period of time to occur, sometimes growth in BDSM is very quick. Take someone who is into flogging, for example. They may have started out their BDSM journey receiving light floggings and avoiding anything to do with blood, bruising or marking. Fast-forward a few months and you might find them involved in the heaviest caning or flogging scenes and being left with bruises and weals which last for days. What has changed in that short time?

Have they become enlightened? Have they changed in some profound way? Has their physiology morphed in those few short months so that now they are extra-human?

What's happened is that they have learned about themselves. They haven't fundamentally changed, but what they thought they were, what limits they thought they had, has been replaced by a better understanding of themselves.

One could say that what they thought they were, and what limits they thought they had at the start of their BDSM journey were not real or were possibly incomplete. If the poundings that they take now are profoundly satisfying, what were the quick stings and tickles those few months ago? Perhaps they were licentious hints of what was to come.

We could argue that if what they are doing now is right for them, then what they were doing a few months ago wasn't. Those few months ago they were experiencing what they thought they needed or wanted, but it was all aimed at a false or incomplete image of themselves. And because it was aimed at a false image it was probably not fully satisfying.

It may have been new, exciting and thrilling, and this can sometimes pass for something profound. But being merely new, exciting and thrilling rarely satisfies for long. To be profoundly satisfying and fulfilling it needs to be aimed at the real person and at their real needs, not at an illusion, false image, or idealised presentation.

# 8.14   Unconscious limits

When we talk about limits in BDSM, most people think of the sorts of limits which get negotiated before a scene. For example, a bottom may tell her top that she doesn't want rope marks or rope burns, doesn't want any bruising except on her butt, and that she doesn't agree to unprotected sex. These are her limits for the scene.

Limits provide protection. For example, no bruises or marks except on the butt might be necessary for a woman who works as a model, or for a guy who plans on going to the beach the next day with vanilla friends who aren't aware of his BDSM inclinations. This sort of limit protects them from embarrassment, awkward explanations, or even social rejection.

Someone might have other limits because they find an activity terrifying, against their beliefs, just plain unpleasant, or because they have legitimate medical concerns, such as an allergy or a fear of infection.

As someone gets more experienced or skilled in BDSM activities, or as they become more comfortable with their own reactions or with their partner, they may refine their limits. They may look for more intensity and risk the marks, or they may schedule some of their activities so that any marks will have faded by the time they need to show the affected parts of their bodies to others.

A certain respectful awareness of your own weaknesses, strengths, and background can help you to create useful and effective limits. While bruises and abrasions are obvious limits for some people, less obvious limits—such as avoiding play rape scenes for someone who was abused as a child—are important to others.

Up to this point I've been talking about conscious limits, about the rational choices we make to protect something we're fully aware might be at risk.

Many people, on the other hand, will automatically and unconsciously avoid some activities—both in their vanilla and BDSM lives—-which present some sort of risk or threat, and they'll automatically and unconsciously embrace other activities which are safe and reassuring. They do this without consciously thinking about it. Their unconscious mind guides their choices in such a way as to keep them safe. For example, someone who was raped or abused as a child may unconsciously and automatically avoid situations which have the potential to remind them of what they went through such as being tied up in particular circumstances, the use of knives on them, verbal threats, and so on.

In an ideal world we'd be able to discuss all of our limits with our partners, and we'd negotiate with them and agree on what's in and what's out. But what about unconscious limits? What about the choices our unconscious mind makes which we're not aware of?

One of the ways the unconscious can get involved with and interfere with our BDSM is in our choice of partners. It can push us towards choosing a partner who simply can't cause our limits to be breached because they are either physically or psychologically incapable in some way.

## Someone who is physically incapable

Let us suppose we're talking about a submissive who is afraid of surrendering, or who has had an unfortunate experience with a top in the past who physically harmed her through an unsafe flogging. Her unconscious mind may push her towards choosing someone who has some physical or medical handicap as her next top or dominant. This is a very effective way of ensuring that her limits will never be exceeded.

For example, she may choose a dominant or top who is extremely unfit or overweight. They are unlikely to ever place any physical demands on her. They're not going to be able to engage in heavy or intense flogging scenes because they don't have the stamina or energy for it. Likewise, unless she is very tiny, they're not going to be able to haul her around and do physically challenging scenes such as suspension bondage or intense military interrogations with her.

She can still do whatever her dominant or top wants while being safe in the unconscious knowledge that he won't be able to get anywhere near her limits. For her unconscious this is a win-win situation because she gets to be as submissive and compliant as possible while never getting near anything that her unconscious considers unsafe.

You might think that this sort of situation is not 100% guaranteed to protect her. For example, what happens if her top enlists the aid of another, fitter top to help out in a more demanding scene? With this extra horsepower shouldn't she be facing the same sort of risk her unconscious was trying to avoid?

At first glance, this might seem true, but this is the unconscious mind we're talking about here, and it has an answer. This situation is easily defeated by her unconscious insisting that she's shy or embarrassed in front of others, or that she is just a "one-man woman" and will only play with her top. Her kind and considerate dominant will never force her to do something she doesn't like and so she's safe.

*Recognising pitfalls and obstacles*

Medical problems—such as blindness, diabetes, heart conditions, asthma, and even allergies—can also create physical limitations for some tops and dominants which a submissive can unconsciously exploit. While the submissive can say they are up for anything, by choosing such a limited partner they have created a situation where their dominant's own physical limits protect the submissive from getting anywhere which the submissive unconsciously thinks is unsafe.

This behaviour of unconsciously choosing a partner with physical limitations has D&s ramifications because the submissive's unconscious mind has already taken control of much of the shape of the couple's BDSM relationship and there isn't really anything the top or dominant can do about it, even if he is aware of it... which is probably unlikely.

It isn't just submissives who make such unconscious choices like this. Dominants can also unconsciously choose partners with physical limitations so that they don't have to go into certain areas or perform certain activities which they feel uncomfortable with or which they find challenging. For example, a dominant who lacks confidence in his flogging ability, who lacks strength in his arm, or who doesn't have a lot of stamina, might be attracted to a submissive who has back problems. His unconscious might tell him that her charm, wit, intelligence, or ability to go into sub-space are highly attractive and this gives him an excuse to avoid flogging almost completely. It may be that she's not really that attractive after all, but if his unconscious mind pushes hard enough he'll come to think she is and this protects him from having to confront his shortcomings.

## Someone who is intellectually or emotionally incapable

When we stray into the areas of BDSM which are less physical and more intellectual or psychological such as D&s or M/s, then a very effective way for a submissive to unconsciously ensure that she isn't dominated more than she's comfortable with is simply to pick a partner who isn't as experienced or as smart as she is.

This works for a submissive or bottom who is, for example, keen on the physical side of BDSM—the floggings, canings, piercings and bondage—but who unconsciously doesn't want anyone who can psychologically dominate her. Thus, a muscle man with limited brains who can barely string two grunts together may seem very attractive to her. He can certainly push her physical buttons, and at the same time she can manipulate him fairly easily so that he thinks he is getting the whole D&s package when he is actually only getting the wrapping.

The unconscious mind can be quite subtle, and a dominant may not even realise that he or she is in a situation where they are being manipulated by the clever and devious unconscious of their submissive partner. In the present example, this unconscious is aiming to allow the submissive any number of physical experiences, and at the same time is protecting her from being dominated or controlled psychologically. Surrender is probably an element in this. Psychological surrender is sometimes more threatening than physical surrender and is potentially easier to avoid—and stay safe from—if the submissive is smarter, quicker, or more experienced than the dominant.

*Recognising pitfalls and obstacles*

The dominant may even think how lucky he is to have such a smart submissive at his beck and call!

Like all the unconscious limits I am talking about here, a dominant can create or impose them just as much as a submissive. For example, a dominant who is unconsciously insecure may pick a submissive who is intellectually his inferior and thus be certain both of his ability to dominate and of her inability to resist.

In contrast, for someone who is looking for the experience of actually controlling his partner, having control provided on a platter in the form of a submissive who simply cannot provide any resistance can take much of the excitement away because there is little challenge and, importantly, little penetration with them.

## Someone who is geographically incapable

There are all sorts of BDSM connections and activities which truly flower when there is long-term, ongoing, and continuous contact between two people. Profound explorations of control are a good example, and these can be found in some forms of D&s and M/s. For these to be successful, it generally needs the people involved to be together frequently such as when they live together or work together in the same small office or local area. This extended contact creates the opportunity for deep control to be imposed, developed and enjoyed.

This isn't going to happen for people who don't live or work together or who live in different cities. A submissive who only sees her dominant every second weekend will still need to retain extensive authority over her life. She'll have to earn money without her dominant being involved. She'll have to do shopping, prepare food for herself, clean her apartment, make important life choices, plan her financial future and retirement, and deal with all sorts of day-to-day issues without him. This isn't because he can't give her direction, but with him having such a tiny involvement in her life he can't actually make effective decisions because he simply doesn't have the awareness of her life to do so.

So, for a submissive or slave who wants only to experience superficial control and surrender, or who is unconsciously afraid of experiencing anything more, picking a partner who can only have a long-distance relationship can be ideal. Someone who lives in a different city, or who is perhaps in the military and is away frequently, is perfect.

It's worth considering that on-line BDSM relationships can fit into this sort of geographical incapability. Internet-based, real-time chat offers a chance for people to engage in limited forms of D&s or M/s, but the same sorts of limitations apply here as they do with geographically distant partners. Time spent facing each other from behind the glass screens is limited. It may be that the two people involved really only have an understanding of what they can see through the camera. Life must go on when each person is away from their screen. Food must be prepared and eaten, clothes bought, bills paid, and so on. The control in such situations may only be transient and shallow without the possibility of anything more.

## Someone who is time incapable

If a submissive enjoys D&s but unconsciously either doesn't want it full time or wants frequent time-outs, a good choice can be to pick a dominant partner who runs their own business—and who, therefore, often works late—or a dominant who has children who either live with them or who they see frequently.

Business and family frequently create times when BDSM simply can't be done. While Sir Diddums might still be the master or dominant when the kids are around, he's not going to be in a position to have his submissive crawl around on all fours in front of them. This can be her respite from anything too intense.

A dominant might also unconsciously choose a submissive who has time constraints because it can limit how much responsibility he needs to shoulder. If the submissive works in an area of emergency services and might get called out to work at any time, it means the dominant escapes having to do intense scenes because their submissive must be ready to go to work and deal with other people's traumas at any time. They can't be in a state that needs too many bandages or too much aftercare.

## Problems with this strategy

The big problem with consciously or unconsciously picking a partner who is actually incapable of pushing your limits today is that he or she will be just as incapable of pushing them tomorrow, next month, or next year. When you reach a point where you want to increase your limits and look for more variety, intensity or challenge, your limited partner can't go with you. The only real choice you have is either to abandon your BDSM and personal growth and stay with them—which may be necessary if you have set up a family or had kids with them, or give up your partner and move on to someone else who has fewer inherent limits.

Avoiding having to make this choice sounds deceptively easy: pick a partner who can grow with you. However, if you find yourself attracted to someone who is clearly inferior, who is somehow or sometimes unavailable, or who is lacking in some important areas—such as health, fitness, wit, cleverness, or IQ—then you really should be asking yourself what you see in them and what sort of future you can have with them. Your unconscious mind reacts to the here-and-now. It may be pushing you towards someone who is "safe" today, but who may not be able to keep you company on your BDSM journey in the long term.

## 8.15  Avoiding surrender

An important part of BDSM is being engaged by your partner and being engaged by them, but for this to happen you need to open yourself up to what they do, and they need to open themselves up to what you do.

I need to digress for a moment here because I have a little linguistic problem. I want to talk about surrender and "limited surrender", but some dictionary definitions and some writers on the subject of surrender consider surrender to be absolute and that you can't surrender in a limited way. When you hold something back, they instead call this "submission". This is a very important distinction, and it's one I need to make and use in the following paragraphs. Unfortunately, the term "submission" has a different connotation for many people into BDSM and I don't want my use of it here to cause confusion or offence by implying that what they do and how they label themselves is in any way inferior.

*Recognising pitfalls and obstacles*

So for the moment, when you open yourself up completely to the experience I'll call it surrender. When you only open yourself up in a limited way, trying to keep control of the experience, I'll call it submitting or submission. You'll see why I want this distinction imminently.

Submitting is sometimes a preferred option to surrender. Suppose you know that after a few taps of a flogger your inhibitions go out the door and you're anyone's. Clearly, being anyone's is not a safe thing all the time, especially with a new partner who you don't know and can't fully trust. However, you may like being tapped with a flogger even without getting to the point of being anyone's. This means that with someone you've just met at a BDSM play party you need to stop the flogging action before you reach the critical point. Part of you needs to hold back and keep a supervisory eye on what's happening so that you can say your safe word, wave a red flag, or whatever, at the necessary time. This means you can't completely surrender to the experience. You need to hold something back for the duration of the scene.

There are many other times and reasons when submitting, rather than surrendering, is the best option. For example:

- When you only have a limited amount of time and you need to keep an eye on the clock,

- When there are kids, family, or others nearby and you've got to limit how much noise you make,

- When you or your partner are trying something new and don't know quite how it's going to work out, and

- When you're with someone new and you don't want them to see how truly weird you are until you know they can handle it.

It might seem that this discussion of surrender versus submission applies primarily to the folk on the receiving end of the cane or flogger, or to the ones being tied or humiliated, or to those who provide personal or sexual service to their partners. This isn't true. A master, top, or dominant can equally be in the position of needing to choose between submitting to the experience they are having with their partner or surrendering to it. For example, a top who is flogging a relatively new partner needs to pay close attention to the reactions of this bottom in case they become overwhelmed, distressed, or simply reach a physical limit such as starting to bleed. The top can't completely surrender to this shared experience because he needs to be ready to stop or change what he's doing at any time. On the other hand, if this top is flogging a partner with "leather skin"[3] he doesn't need to be on guard to such an extent and can really let himself go in terms of how hard he hits and for how long. He can surrender fully to the experience.

So all of this discussion about surrender applies equally well to masters, slaves, dominants, submissives, tops, and bottoms. By holding back for any reason, you can't fully immerse yourself into what's going on between you and your partner. You can't surrender to it.

All of the situations I've mentioned so far are good reasons to hold back. You know what's going on, you understand the situation, and you make the choice to proceed with engaging

---

[3] The term "leather skin" is sometimes used to refer to someone who has been flogged so often that their skin has adapted and become toughened. They can endure and embrace long, intense floggings with minimal bruising, redness, or abrasion.

*Recognising pitfalls and obstacles*

your partner BDSM-wise knowing that you have to hold back. This is a conscious choice.

However, some people will hold back unconsciously. It's often fear of one sort or another. They may have problems with being intimate and therefore won't open the door all the way to you and what you're doing with them, or they'll stand at the door ready to push you out and slam it shut at a moment's notice. Others may have been hurt in the past and the fear they learned back then stops them being open now. They can't immerse themselves in the BDSM experience completely because part of them is afraid and is unconsciously holding themselves back.

## Strategies

People who unconsciously avoid surrender often have some interesting strategies to achieve this. For example:

- They may only play at parties. This is quite effective because play at a BDSM party is unlikely to be too intimate. Scenes at play parties are usually limited to about half an hour or so due to others wanting to use the play equipment or dungeon. Also, play at most parties tends to be conservative and this avoids anything too challenging, too intense, or too risky.

- They only agree to particular types of activity which don't risk surrender being triggered. Some types of scene compel surrender; it's unavoidable. For example, while you might gird your loins, endure a flogging, and not surrender, with some scenes involving intense stimulation or pain—such as cutting—no amount of girding is going to help you resist the pain forever. You must surrender to it eventually. By not getting involved with such scenes in the first place you can avoid surrender.

I hasten to add here that just because someone doesn't like intense pain or cutting it doesn't mean they're avoiding surrender. It might simply be something which doesn't have a positive outcome for them. For others for whom it is a doorway to intense and positive surrender, it can be something which they only do with someone they trust.

- They physically close their eyes so that they can be in their own little world and not have to see or face their partner. They may surrender to the physical feelings and sensations, but by closing their eyes they can exclude their partner from this experience. This means that they can avoid the risk of the bonding which can occur through the shared intensity or power of their BDSM experiences.

Following on from an earlier discussion, two other effective strategies someone might use to avoid surrender in a D&s context, as opposed to a physical play context, are:

- To unconsciously choose a partner who simply cannot physically or mentally dominate them, or

- To choose a situation where they can't be completely dominated such as only playing at D&s at a party where time is limited.

## Questions

1. Are there any activities you avoid—either as a dominant, top, submissive, bottom, etc.—because you feel nervous

about them even though they are, in themselves,
technically quite safe?

2. Are there activities which make you uncomfortable for no
   obvious reason?

3. Are there activities or times when you feel yourself
   completely open to your partner, to what they're doing,
   and to where it's taking you?

4. Are there people who you can be more open with than
   others? What's the difference?

## 8.16   Being worshipped

I don't mind being worshipped. It can be a very nice thing.
One of the key parts of a BDSM relationship is power disparity
and the power disparity must be used or manifested to have any
effect. Worship is a way in which each partner gets to represent
or enact that power differential. The submissive or slave gets
to lower themselves, debase themselves, or grovel below their
master, mistress or dominant, while their master, mistress or
dominant gets to stand over or take a place above their partner.
Worship can and does allow the status or rank of each partner to
be concretely played out. The way each person behaves clearly
identifies one partner as being dominant or higher ranked, while
the other is submissive or lower ranked.

This can be a good thing. For example, when worship is used to
reinforce rank or role, or when it's used as a way to express the
power the dominant or master has over their partner—such as
by compelling the submissive to their knees, or to require them

to kiss or lick their dominant's boots—this can be very effective and empowering.

However, worship can also be twisted into a bad thing such as when the dominant or master is *required* by their submissive to behave, or dress, or speak in particular ways to remain "worship-able"; then it becomes one-way and manipulative of the dominant or master. This can happen without the dominant being aware, and it means that the submissive is the one doing the controlling. This is not uncommon.

At first glance, being idolised might seem like a very nice thing for a dominant. It can seem quite complimentary and a boost for your ego to be put on a pedestal and treated as if the very ground you walk upon is sacred.

It is however, hard being an idol. For a start, you have to be available whenever your worshippers want to worship you. You don't get to set the schedule. They do. And like other idols you might not actually get anything from your worshippers. Many worshipful submissives are looking for a dominant who doesn't actually do anything except basically stand there, "look like a dom," and maybe occasionally wave a flogger or tie a knot. Being an idol means you have to maintain certain standards. Your submissive or slave may even demand it. If your halo drops, if you have a late night out on the turps and look a bit worse for wear in the morning, or if you don't dress to their standards, your worshipper will not be happy because you're not living up to the standard they require. They'll even get pissed off with you because you've damaged the image they need you to maintain and because you have, they feel, taken away their object of worship. In effect, you've descended from the pedestal they put you on without their permission.

This, I think, explains why the original gods and buddhas long ago moved on and left behind carved or sculpted statues in their place. Statues never let worshippers down. In fact, the worshippers construct them that way. The statues always have their hair in place, never have bad days, and can be constantly happy, jolly fellows—religion permitting.

A submissive or slave who approaches you AND who is all bubbling and effusive in their praise of you and your wonderfulness AND who insists on grovelling at your feet or worshipping you is someone to be wary of. There's nothing wrong with someone thinking that you're wonderful and amazing because you actually might be that as far as they are concerned. It is the worshipping and grovelling bit where things can go astray because these can easily become one-way. For someone to grovel at your feet, for example, you need either to be standing still or posing majestically instead of doing something you'd rather be doing. You stand still, you let your submissive grovel at your feet, and you're doing them a favour. It might even cost you because as well as the time lost, later on you'll have to clean the saliva trails off your shoes.

On the other hand, someone who thinks you're amazing and would like to spend time with you, maybe attend you or serve you, fetch you drinks and such like, could genuinely be trying to learn from you, or enjoy your skills and abilities, and give you something in return.

This idea of being compelled to maintain an image is, in itself, not a bad thing if it's open and honest. A worship-based relationship needs to be two-way, just like any other relationship in BDSM. Worshipping must be done as an adult. Worshipping your partner should mean that they have your respect as a person, as a dominant, and as your partner in the relationship. The key idea here is "partner" because your relationship is supposed to be mutual with both of you benefitting more-or-less equally.

Needing to present a certain image all the time is a chore, just ask a professional dominatrix. They always have to maintain a certain image, wear particular types of clothes (often uncomfortable if worn for long periods) and act in certain ways, otherwise their customers will stop coming back. They get paid to look and act this way and that is one reward they get out of it. For a dominant in a non-commercial relationship to feel compelled to do the same without compensation is manipulative and one-way.

Putting a dominant or master on a pedestal and worshipping them can also be a defensive move on the part of a submissive or slave. It can be done consciously or unconsciously as a way of creating distance between them and their master/dominant in a similar way to the strategies I discussed in section 8.14, *Unconscious limits*. As long as the dominant feels compelled to remain on the pedestal, they can't actually get down, become mortal, and fully engage their submissive or slave. This ensures that there always will be distance between the two of them. And if the submissive isn't feeling consciously or unconsciously safe enough, they just worship and grovel a bit more and thereby move their dominant to a taller pedestal.

This can all happen the other way around as well. If a dominant or master insists that his slave or submissive worships him all the time, or that they treat him like a minor god, it could be that he is trying to place distance between himself and his submissive or that he is trying to create a barrier to prevent getting too involved.

Although I'm focussing on the abuse of worship here, I would like to stress that worship can be a useful part of a BDSM relationship. It does reinforce rank, which can be very effective, and it can be helpful in maintaining distance when distance is needed. There's a saying that "familiarity breeds contempt" and it means that by getting to close or knowing too much about someone that they are lowered in your eyes. This may not be a good thing in some BDSM relationships and encouraging or even requiring worship can help prevent this... assuming that the dominant behaves in a way which merits worship, of course.

Worship is also a good tool where distance must be maintained for other reasons, such as in a part-time BDSM relationship where the people involved have other interests or obligations and can't do 24/7 BDSM. In this case, using a worship as a behavioural way of not getting too close can be excellent.

Worship can be a situation which leads to lack of engagement. If your partner metaphorically thinks that the Sun shines out of your rear end... well, it's obvious that it doesn't and if they're labouring under the illusion that it does then they're not engaging you. To have a strong and healthy relationship they need to be dealing with the real you. This is something I discussed right at the beginning of book one of this series. If they're interacting with someone who has solar radiation coming out of their butt hole then clearly they're not interacting with you. They're interacting with someone who they're imagining and even though this imaginary person might look like you, wear the same clothes as you, and be standing in the same spot you are, it's not you.

## Questions and discussion

For submissives and slaves:

- When you worship your dominant, or when you kneel or grovel at their feet, what do they get out of it?

- You might find it very powerful, but what benefit, reward, satisfaction, or pleasure, do they get then and there?

- How does your worship actually help them meet their own needs?

- Is there something your dominant or master could do, or stop doing, which would make it difficult or impossible for you to continue worshipping them? How would this effect your relationship?

- Do you serve your master or dominant? What relationship does your service have to worship?

For dominants and masters:

- Do you find that you need to maintain a certain image or certain standards for your submissive? Is this a burden?

- If you enjoy being worshipped, what is it that you find satisfying or rewarding?

  - Is it the implicit flattery?

  - Is the way they worship you physically or sexually exciting or pleasing?

  - Is it what happens after the worship?

- Does your submissive or slave serve you? How do they serve you, and is there any relationship between their service and their worship? If they no longer worshipped you, would the service continue? Would it change?

*Recognising pitfalls and obstacles*

## 8.17    Avoiding responsibility

There are some folk who enter into the world of BDSM—particularly in areas such as D&s or M/s—who are there because they don't want to be answerable either for themselves, for their lives, or for much of what goes on around them.

They style themselves as submissives or slaves and see D&s as a way of handing off as much responsibility as possible to any poor sucker dominant who will take them on. They argue that their dominant takes control and, therefore, takes responsibility so that they—the submissive—can do whatever they want and they're never at fault.

Their dominant, on the other hand, is the one who gets blamed, who cops the flak, or who gets seen as a "bad dominant" who can't keep his submissive out of trouble. Should anyone try to talk to the submissive about any perceived attitude or behaviour problem, the submissive simply refers everything to their dominant: "I belong to Sir Dude and you have to take up any issues about me with him."

Inexperienced dominants can easily be taken in by such submissives. The submissive proclaims that they want or even need to be under the dominant's control and that they'll do whatever they're told. Indeed, at some superficial level they do seem attentive and responsive. The dominant is wooed by the submissive who insists that they are their partner's property, how much they love them, and how much they long to obey and be treasured. This can be very attractive to some dominants.

In reality, the submissive is manipulative and will have a ready supply of legitimate-sounding reasons and excuses for behaving badly or inappropriately. Their dominant will find that they're actually powerless to change their submissive's behaviour. The submissive may act profoundly apologetic if taken to task by their partner, but nothing will change.

These sorts of people exist throughout society. They look for other people to take responsibility for their actions, or they look for ways of denying responsibility for what they do. They aren't confined to BDSM. BDSM though, provides an environment where, on the face of it, someone else actually does take control and responsibility.

Neither responsibility nor answerability are diminished or destroyed in a healthy D&s relationship. What can and does happen is that a submissive makes themselves answerable to their dominant partner. Their dominant acquires the right and duty to set standards, and can insist on obedience and conformity to these standards. Failure leads to discipline or punishment. There is no decrease in responsibility here. On the contrary, responsibility and answerability increase in D&s.

It is not, and never is, the responsibility of a dominant to ensure that their submissive behaves politely, respectfully, and with consideration of others. This is a responsibility which we all have, regardless of whether we are in a BDSM context or not. Trying to invoke the magic phrases, "I'm XYZ's property," or, "I am a submissive," to avoid that responsibility is a good warning sign of someone who doesn't want to be a productive member of society.

## Recognising that this is happening

When these so-called submissives show up they can be difficult to spot. In all likelihood, they've been playing this game—and it is a game—a long time and are very good at getting away with it. More than this, they are very good at getting other people to play their game with them.

Here are some questions to consider:

- Do you feel disempowered in relation to your submissive?

- Do you feel like things are out of your control?

- Do you feel emasculated?

- Do you feel like there's nothing you can do to keep your submissive on the path of good behaviour?

- Do you feel actual fear of what they'll do next?

## Getting out

If you are a dominant involved with such a submissive, here are some important notes:

- Get out. You can't change them. They are experts at what they do. They would have changed a long time ago if they'd wanted to. They will not change for you. This can be a difficult thing for you, as a dominant, to accept, namely that you're powerless to make this person change or do what you want.

- By staying you are enabling them to continue playing this game which is harmful to you and to them.

- While you keep playing their game they are winning, and this is a bad lesson to give them.

## Dominants who avoid responsibility

Nominally it is the tops, dominants and masters who are in control. They are the ones who are supposed to make the decisions, direct the action, and set the priorities. There can be a lot of responsibility tied up in these things.

In purely physical scenes, such as cutting or bondage, there are a number of potential risks including infection, nerve damage, permanent scarring, broken bones or worse. When we start getting into long-term relationships, D&s relationships, M/s relationships and psychological play—such as humiliation, interrogation, and mind fucks—there's scope for emotional damage, trauma, fear, abuse and more.

A dominant, master, or top needs to step up to the plate and be ready to deal with these very possibilities. Sadly, some don't.

Some will say:

- After breath play gone wrong: "I didn't know she had a cold!" or "I didn't know she was asthmatic!"

- After their partner collapses during bondage: "I didn't know he had a blood pressure problem!" or "I didn't know I might need to get him out of the bondage in a hurry!" or "How was I to know the ropes were too tight?"

- After a flogging or whipping scene goes bad: "But she didn't say her safeword!"

- After a surprise play rape scene has a less than happy outcome: "How was I to know she was raped as a child?"

- The day after an intense scene: "How was I to know he might react badly?" or "How could I know that he'd need to talk to me the next day?"

- In general: "It's not my fault! I did everything right!"

The point is that BDSM has risks. While we might talk about SSC[4] or RACK[5], neither these nor any other magic words take away the need for both people involved in any BDSM relationship to take responsibility for what they get into.

For dominant, tops and masters, they need to inform themselves, ask questions, read books, and talk to others before engaging in any activity which might put their partner at risk. In particular, they need to know the physical, emotional, psychological, and skill limits of both themselves and their partner. They need to know what might go wrong and have planned for it.

When you're the top, dominant or master you're often in the best position to prevent things going bad. Not taking advantage of that position to do so is irresponsible.

And if your partner is the top, dominant or master in your relationship and they avoid taking responsibility, find the nearest door and use it.

---

[4] A common BDSM motto: Safe, Sane and Consensual.

[5] Another common BDSM motto: Risk-Aware Consensual Kink.

# Chapter 9

# Pushing the kinky sex line

In book one of this series, *Understanding BDSM Relationships*, I have a chapter called *Uncomfortable thoughts*, and one of the things I talk about in it is how some people dress their BDSM as kinky sex to make it more acceptable, often to themselves.

Even someone who is not very conservative can have trouble with the ideas that they like being hit or hurt by their partner, or that their partner likes hitting them or hurting them. The general idea in our society, in many families, and in many religions, is that you don't go around hitting people, especially someone you care about deeply. There are even laws which say hitting and hurting people can land you in prison. These attitudes generally encourage us to think of being hit or hurt as something which we shouldn't accept.

On the other hand, and particularly over the last few decades, sex—and even casual sex—has become more acceptable, more widely discussed, and even anticipated between two people who have only barely just met.

On top of this, it's easy to link our BDSM play and sex play. There are forms of BDSM which don't involve pain or ropes—such as sensation play or wax play—which can be quite sensual. It's one thing to talk about dripping hot wax on to someone, which can sound like a medieval torture, and quite another to describe dripping cooling wax onto our naked partner's nipples and then sensually peeling it off with our fingernails once it has set. The latter clearly sounds sexy while the former perhaps sounds pathological!

Sex shops invite bondage play between innocents when they sell the now-famous, fluffy pink handcuffs. The fact that we can buy them in sex shops means they must have something to do with sex, and the fact that using them is "about sex" makes the BDSM part more acceptable.

Heavier forms of BDSM, such as flogging or rope bondage, also become more acceptable if they don't involve blood, do involve nudity, and end with sex.

But as we have seen through the course of this series of books, hitting someone, tying them up, humiliating them, ordering them around, injuring them, bruising them, and so on, even when there's no sex in sight, can be positive, constructive and life-affirming for two people in many, many ways.

This all means that for many people exploring BDSM there is a line to cross, and that line separates seeing BDSM as kinky sex, and seeing some or all of BDSM as being quite distinct from sex. While you try to see BDSM as merely kinky sex then you can't see what might be positive aspects of BDSM without sex. If your BDSM play always needs to involve nudity, sex, or orgasms, then it can be hard to find some of the forms of surrender or catharsis which many other people look for and achieve in their BDSM.

Dominant and submissive relationships, and master/slave relationships, can especially become restricted and highly limited if you can or will only see BDSM in terms of sex. Topping and bottoming are typically scene-based, and these are quite amenable to being done in a one-on-one or sexual context such as in a bedroom or *sans* clothes in a dungeon. But D&s and M/s often extend outside of the dungeon or bedroom and for much or all of the time may be non-sexual. Embracing the idea that BDSM need not be about sex can liberate D&s and M/s relationships.

Going even further, when you can completely separate yourself from the idea that BDSM is about sex, it means that you can freely see which wants and needs you and your partner have which can or should be done without sex, and those which are compatible with sex. Sometimes sex can get in the way of meeting needs when it, and not the need, is the focus. But at other times, such as when BDSM is used for recreation, sex can be part of the play without interfering.

However, going back to acceptability for a moment, because we aren't encouraged by society to think of hurt, pain and restraint as acceptable, it can be that we simply don't think about them and whether they are important to us or to our partner. And because they may never come to mind we might not consciously realise that there is more than kinky sex going on in our BDSM, even when what we do is already heading in that direction.

It's worthwhile then, especially for people who have been actively exploring BDSM for more than a short while, to periodically reflect on what they enjoy doing, the role of sex, and especially the role of things other than sex. Because there can be so much going on in BDSM, with so many different motivations, wants and needs involved, teasing out the individual aspects which are important and making sure they are addressed can make what we do much more satisfying and rewarding for us and our partners.

# Chapter 10

# Incomplete needs meeting

As we've seen throughout this series of books, BDSM is often about exploring and satisfying wants and needs which aren't always obvious. Certainly, some of the reasons why people do BDSM can be quite private and intimate, and for this reason they won't always communicate what they're pursuing to their partner unless they trust their partner completely... and sometimes not even then.

When two BDSM folk get together for a casual encounter it's implicit that what they do together must be satisfying, rewarding, or exciting for both of them. If one has to put in a lot of effort to satisfy their casual partner and doesn't get enough back then it's not worth their while to get involved in the first place. But in a longer-term relationship it doesn't need to be this way. Because there are going to be regular BDSM encounters between the two people involved it means that there doesn't need to be this per-scene balance that casual play tends to require. One partner can afford to devote themselves in one scene to the needs of their partner knowing that this will be balanced in the future.

This is particularly relevant because some of the needs which BDSM can satisfy are explicitly one-sided anyway. For example, and as I've already noted earlier, there can be a physiological release associated with tight rope bondage. This typically involves a comfortably-positioned submissive or bottom in a tight, full-body rope tie. Once tied they need to be quietly monitored for 15 minutes or so. This can be profoundly relaxing, a deep release and very calming for the submissive. Obviously, for the top who tied them up it's not very engaging. They need to just sit around, keep an eye on their tied partner, and then release them once the time is up.

There's a not-so-obvious aspect to this, which is that if you tie your partner up for such a session and then untie them too early you may end up with them feeling very irritable or less satisfied than when you started. Many BDSM activities can be like this. Too little or too much can be worse than nothing at all. Pain play, such as cutting, generally needs a certain amount of pain for a certain amount of time in a certain environment (e.g., quiet, alone with partner, warm, no music) to be effective. The wrong sort of pain, or too much pain, or too little pain, or pain which goes on for too long, or pain which doesn't go on for long enough, or the wrong environment may not lead to the necessary emotional or psychological release.

The rhythmic thudding of heavy flogging can take a submissive or bottom into what's called sub-space, which is quite relaxing and can be cathartic, but it can take time to get there and if

*Incomplete needs meeting*

you stop flogging too early they may end up, again, irritable or unsatisfied. If you flog too long or too hard then they may also end up only half-way there.

Part of the irritation can come from the let down. If someone has been looking forward to a satisfying scene with their partner and the scene is cut short before their needs are fully met, or if the scene doesn't go the way it usually does—such as when their partner surprises them by trying something new—then needs also might not get met. It can mean waiting for another day or another week to try again.

More than this though is that an incomplete needs-meeting session or scene can create an additional problem rather than solve one. What do you do with half a catharsis, for example? Or if someone is looking for that physiological release associated with a tight bondage tie and they're untied too early, what do they do with half a physiological release? Someone who uses the stimulation, the pain, the impacts, the restraint, and the interaction with their partner to get to a certain mental state is going to follow a particular path to get there. If the stimulation stops too soon, then they end up stuck part way along the path, neither at the beginning nor the end. It can leave them in a sensitive or vulnerable state for hours, days, or longer.

Dominants and tops, too, need their release and where a dominant uses a BDSM activity for this, their submissive partner also needs to be able to go the distance. This can be apparent when a dominant uses a heavy activity, such as a long and strenuous flogging, to get built-up nervous energy out of his system. If his submissive partner is unable to endure the flogging and needs to stop early, then the dominant can be left feeling unsatisfied and with energy left that he doesn't want and can't get rid of.

A top or dominant who uses BDSM as an opportunity for self expression—such as through artistic rope work, or creative needle play—can also be left hanging and unsatisfied if he doesn't get to finish what he started because of an interruption or if his partner calls it off early.

Regardless of whether you are a top, bottom, dominant or submissive, it may not be obvious to you when your partner is using the activities you share to achieve such an internal catharsis, some sort emotional release, or some other profound outcome. You should talk to them to make sure that their needs are being met. You need to know—and this, of course, has to do with engagement—when they have wants or needs which they satisfy with you through BDSM, what they need to do or what you need to do for this to happen, and when it's enough.

When you are a bottom or submissive it can be useful to devise a system of signals, possibly hand signals, which tell your partner of your changing needs throughout such a scene. For example, you might have a signal for "Harder!", or for "Slower!", or for "Stop! Now I need to be quiet for while." These can help your partner help you navigate through your own internal feelings using what they do with you while distracting you as little as possible.

What we're talking about here is meeting needs, and in the context of a longer-term relationship needs meeting can take on a whole different shape to what's possible in casual encounters. When profound needs or profound forms of release are being sought, a longer-term relationship can provide times when only the needs of one partner are addressed and this focus means that the needs can be met much more deeply than in a casual encounter. Also, a longer-term relationship allows each person to learn their partner's particular needs intimately, to learn what triggers them, and how to help meet those needs.

This point about engagement and knowing your partner's needs can be quite important because if someone does have a strong need and they try to get it satisfied with someone who doesn't know them well, or who doesn't know about this need, and the two of them do some sort of scene together, then there's a risk that the person without the strong need will be focusing on having a good time or on getting what they want out of it, while the person with the strong need may end up being left high and dry when their partner reaches their own desired level of satisfaction and stops.

A benefit of a longer-term relationship is that you can focus on one need, meet it fully, and then at some later time visit other wants, needs and lusts. Particularly where one partner has stronger BDSM needs than the other, or where they both have strong needs but which are satisfied in entirely different ways, recognising that there must be some times put aside for focused needs meeting and then other times which can be used for fun, bonding, sex, recreation, or whatever, can avoid one or other partner being left unsated.

# Chapter 11

# False righteousness

One of the problems which afflicts BDSM generally, and which affects BDSM relationships in a particularly negative way, is false righteousness. The Oxford English Dictionary[1] defines righteousness as:

> righteousness, *n.  The state or quality of being righteous or just; conformity to the precepts of divine law or accepted standards of morality; uprightness, rectitude; virtue, integrity.*

False righteousness is having the absolute conviction that what you are doing is right when it isn't. More than this, it also extends to conveying this conviction to others.

---

[1] [OED]

In the BDSM world, false righteousness typically develops in individuals and groups as a result of isolation. I've already noted one form of isolation a number of times through this series of books, and that is the isolation which society-in-general imposes on us through lack of acceptance of BDSM and its practices. This social isolation means that some people develop their BDSM interests and understanding in hidden geographical pockets with little or no contact with other BDSM enthusiasts.

With no yardsticks against which to measure their understanding, skills or abilities, these people can come to believe that what they're doing is good, safe, healthy or productive simply because in their limited experience or in their own small social group it all seems to be going smashingly. Indeed, it might be going smashingly simply because through luck they haven't encountered any problems and what they do is, in fact, quite risky.

I'm reminded of such a situation where a gathering of BDSM practitioners from all across the state was organised for the first time in a number of years. This gathering lasted a whole weekend and was an opportunity for people to demonstrate, share, and discuss their interests. One demonstration was from a top who lived in a small town which had just a handful of enthusiasts. He wanted to demonstrate fire play. This involves wiping a cloth or swab soaked in a volatile liquid—such as an alcohol/water mix—across a small patch of a bottom's skin, setting fire to the vapour, and then quickly extinguishing it to prevent their skin from getting too hot. This can have a powerful psychological effect on a bottom because it looks and feels like they are on fire when it is not actually their skin which burns, but the vapour above their skin instead.

Anyway, this top got his bottom, a well-endowed and very "forward" young female, to sit topless in a chair and then he wet the top of one of her breasts with the volatile liquid and set it alight. A small plume of flame rose from her boob as expected, and he quickly put it out. A number of other tops in the audience then immediately stopped his demonstration for safety reasons.

There were two problems. Firstly, done the way he did it there's a serious risk that flames rising up towards the bottom's face can get inhaled and damage nasal passages, throat or lungs. Secondly, hair can easily catch fire and while this particular bottom's hair was quite short, long hair can hang down towards the breasts and it invites future disaster to demonstrate such a risky way of doing fire play to an audience which contained inexperienced BDSM folk who then might go home and try it on someone with long hair.

This top had learned his fire play skills in isolation, and because he had successfully set fire to a number of people without problems, he had come to believe that what he was doing was right. It only needed for him to try this "seated fire play" with a bit too much alcohol, or with too much delay in putting out the flame, or with someone with long hair, or with someone who breathed in at the wrong time, and he might have had a major medical problem on his hands.

This same sort of skills problem can develop in a number of areas of BDSM such as flogging, caning, suspension bondage, and so on. While light-and-fluffy play is often fairly safe, when overconfidence develops in isolation, people can be taking risks which they don't appreciate and can be getting themselves into serious trouble.

Isolation and lack of shared experience also leads to a false righteousness in attitudes and beliefs. This is something which we can sometimes see in *The gift of submission* which I discussed in detail back in section 7.11 on page 56. A submissive who experiences intense submissive feelings or intense feelings of surrender for the first time may not have the experience or understanding to be able to correctly and realistically deal with these feelings. Because they may never have heard of these feelings before, they may think of them as special or magical and might come up with romantic or impractical theories to understand and handle them. With no one around to tell them otherwise, these ideas may become entrenched and even graduate to being "obvious". Similarly, a submissive who has been raised on the BDSM equivalent of Mills & Boon novels[2] may have completely unrealistic ideas of how BDSM relationships actually play out and may bring these hard-to-change ideas with them when they set up shop with a dominant. Dominants, of course, aren't immune to this. Literature such as *The Story Of O*[3] can easily give them the wrong impression about what to do with a submissive or bottom and lead them to extremes which the average bottom or submissive might never survive, let alone endure.

I'm reminded of some strong-minded young female virgins here because many of them inflict this same sort of righteousness on their first boyfriends. A female friend with whom I was discussing this commented that sex changes a woman. When she becomes sexually active, she behaves differently and has different values than a virgin. Similarly, BDSM experience changes both a dominant and a submissive. It might be that they

---

[2] A famous line of hundreds (thousands?) of escapist, romance-heavy novels from Britain - see http://en.wikipedia.org/wiki/Mills_%26_Boon

[3] [REAGE1954]

*False righteousness*

don't get the full idea until they have had a couple of partners, but the same can probably be said about virgins, too.

Righteousness can develop entirely out of ignorance, but often ego has a place in holding on to it. Someone who has devoted a lot of time to practicing what they think is right may react badly if they start to get the idea that they may not be so right after all. They may go to extreme lengths both to avoid being educated and to avoid contact with those who might be better informed. They might avoid going to workshops or reading books about BDSM, and may attempt to encourage others around them to similarly isolate themselves. All this to ensure that their own standing, and any power or influence they wield in their local group is not diminished. This applies to submissives just as much as it does to dominants because in a small pond it's easy to be a big fish, and being a big fish means you have social standing. If the pond suddenly becomes bigger through an influx of knowledge or through an influx of people with better skills, the previously big fish might end up looking fairly small and lose their social position.

When it exists, false righteousness creates an artificial foundation for a relationship. In book one of this series I described three characteristics of BDSM relationships—disparity of power, penetration, and engagement—and referred to them as pillars. These pillars support a BDSM relationship and implicitly they must rest on a solid foundation. If they don't, if the foundation on which they rest is soft and mushy, then it doesn't matter how solid the pillars themselves are. When the foundation is weak then the relationship itself will be precarious and prone to collapse. In the case of false righteousness, this collapse occurs when the foundations begin to shake, typically because of growing knowledge or awareness in or around the people in the relationship.

## 11.1   Entitlement

Along with righteousness can come a sense of entitlement. Entitlement can have to do with anything, but someone who has come to believe that they are a superior dominant or submissive because of their experience can come to expect the social standing I mentioned above, or that their utterances will be treated most seriously, or that they get first pick of any new "meat" which walks in the door of the local monthly BDSM play party, or that their way is clearly the right way.

When they're challenged about any of this they have little to fall back on. Being challenged means that they have to justify or prove themselves, and if they have nothing except their own beliefs or limited experience on which to draw then they may see their little world start to crumble. When there is such a sense of entitlement, they may become loud when challenged or criticised, or may clam up and simply insist they are right and refuse to discuss whatever it is.

*False righteousness*

# Chapter 12

# Conclusion

When we're looking at pitfalls and obstacles to a BDSM relationship then it always will be that we're looking for something going wrong with one or more of the three pillars of BDSM relationships:

- Disparity of power,

- Penetration, or

- Engagement.

A breakdown in any of these three things, or failure of the foundations on which they rest, can change the nature of a relationship, change it from BDSM into plain vanilla, or even bring the relationship to an end. As we've seen in this book, there are many ways in which this can happen.

Communication and trust are always going to be important elements of any relationship and BDSM relationships are no different. However, while vanilla relationships can be less susceptible to problems in these areas and can keep chuffing along even when there are serious communication or trust issues between two people, BDSM is often a lot more sensitive. In particular, engagement is likely to be the first thing to suffer when there is either a communication or a trust problem. As well as creating feelings of distance when engagement diminishes, the depth of our BDSM explorations and their ability to satisfy us and our partners also suffer, often badly.

Another interesting problem which afflicts many BDSM relationships, particularly those involving people new to BDSM, is unrealistic expectations. I mean, *The Story Of O*[1] is a very good read and can be quite a turn-on, but you wouldn't want to try what's in it with a brand new submissive. Many of the things which BDSM and erotic literature tell us are fanciful and often physically dangerous. They make for a good read, but they should stay in books and not venture off the page. Unfortunately, people who are new to BDSM have no way of telling the possible from the unrealistic and may think that what they read can actually be done, or may believe that knights in shining armour (or shiny black leather) are waiting around the corner to carry them off into a world of ecstatic flogging and endless orgasmic delights to which they merely have to surrender. They are in for an unfortunate surprise.

I'm a keen believer both in reality in BDSM and in clearing out any junk which prevents us seeing reality. When there's distance between us and reality, or when we replace reality with fantasy,

---

[1] [REAGE1954]

engagement with our partner suffers. Instead of focussing our energy on what our partner needs, on what we ourselves need, and on what our shared relationship needs, part of our energy goes towards the fantasy and is lost.

First reactions to the realization that a relationship is in crisis, or nearly so, can be denial or to go for a quick fix, such as having more scenes, flogging harder, or going to more workshops. Often however, dealing with a BDSM relationship in crisis can be just a matter of stepping back a bit, then working out what motivations or needs have to be met on both sides, how they have been met in the past, what might be interfering, and how these needs can be met now. It's my hope that this series of books can help you do just that.

# Bibliography

[FERRY2008]         Ferry, Steven M.  *Butlers & Household Managers:  21st Century Professionals.* BookSurge Publishing, 2008.  ISBN 1-4392-0967-7

[MASTERS2008A] Masters, Peter.  *Look Into My Eyes: How To Use Hypnosis To Bring Out The Best In Your Sex Life.* CreateSpace, 2008.  ISBN 1-4404-4986-4

[MASTERS2008]     Masters, Peter.  *This Curious Human Phenomenon:  An exploration of some uncommonly explored aspects of BDSM.* The Nazca Plains Corporation, 2008. ISBN 1-9346-2568-X

[MESTON2007]      Meston, Cindy M. and Buss, David M. *Why Humans Have Sex.*  Archives of Sexual Behaviour, volume 36, no. 4, pages 477 – 507, 2007. ISSN 0004-0002

[OED]  OED. *Oxford English Dictionary (Online Edition).* Oxford University Press, 1989

[REAGE1954]  Reage, Pauline. *The Story Of O.* 1954

# Glossary

24/7        short for 24 hours a day, seven days a week. This
            refers to a type of D&s or M/s relationship where
            the two people involved always interact and engage
            each other in D&s or M/s terms.

BDSM        an acronym for Bondage and Discipline, Domi-
            nance and Submission, and Sadism and Masochism.

Bondage     a BDSM activity where a top, dominant, or master
            uses rope, chain, cuffs or any other method to
            physically restrain their bottom, submissive, or
            slave.

Bottom      a BDSM role. A bottom is the one on the receiving
            end during a BDSM scene such as the one being tied
            up, the one being struck with a flogger, etc.

Cutting     a BDSM activity using very sharp knives or scalpels
            to cut designs into the skin. These can be shallow
            cuts, usually through only a layer or two of skin and
            which are more for psychological effect than to be

actually painful, through to deep cuts which bleed and leave scars.

D&s      a short-hand way to refer to dominant/submissive relationships.

Discipline      any BDSM activity involving an aspect of punishment. Typically things like bare-bottom spanking and caning fall into this category.

Dominant      a BDSM role. A dominant takes charge of some aspect of their partner's activities. This can be solely for the length of a scene, or longer term when they live together.

Dungeon      a special area reserved for BDSM scenes. Usually equipped with specialised and BDSM-adapted furniture such as spanking benches (padded, comfortable benches used during spanking scenes), wooden frames with anchor points used during rope bondage, etc.

Fire play      an activity involving fire, typically where a top applies a thin smear of a volatile liquid—such as an alcohol/water mix—to the skin of a bottom, lights the vapour above the bottom's skin, and then quickly extinguishes the flame to prevent burning.

Flogger      a type of short, multi-tail whip. Usually designed more to thud than sting, the tails are often shorter than one metre and are typically fairly wide and soft. The tails can be made of leather, rope, cord, hair, rubber, etc.

Impact play  any BDSM activities where striking one's partner is the goal. Includes slapping, spanking, paddling, whipping, flogging, and so on.

M/s  a short-hand way to refer to Master/slave relationships.

Master  a BDSM role. A master claims ownership or rights over a slave.

Mistress  a BDSM role. Can be the female counterpart of a master, but often this role is merely a female top.

Mummification  a type of bondage in which the whole body is encased in a form of wrapping in a manner reminiscent of an egyptian mummy (with holes for breathing, of course). Most commonly the material used for wrapping is something like kitchen cling wrap because it's quick and easy to apply.

Needle play  using hypodermic needle tips to thread through the skin, genitals or nipples. Usually done for psychological effect because the needles are actually designed not to hurt (much) unless larger diameters are used. Can also be done for artistic reasons where large numbers of needles are used at one time to create patterns.

Pain play  any BDSM activities where causing sharp or dull pain is the goal. Includes caning, whipping, flogging, cutting, etc.

Paddle  a paddle similar in shape and size to a ping-pong paddle made out of wood or thick leather. Used for paddling, which is similar to spanking but is done with a paddle instead of a hand.

Play party   a type of BDSM event where people get together to engage in BDSM activities and BDSM play with each other. Usually held in a private location, such as someone's home, warehouse, loft, or other dedicated space. Rooms or areas are usually put aside for such play, while other areas are put aside for talking, socialising or eating.

Rope bondage  using rope or cord to physically restrain someone partially or fully. Includes full-body bondage, hog-tying, wrist or ankle cuffs made out of rope, etc.

Scene   a collected series of activities with a BDSM focus having a clearly defined start and end; hence *bondage scene* or *discipline scene*, etc. Often performed in a dungeon.

*Scene* is also sometimes used as a verb meaning to engage in a scene or to perform a scene. For example, *the dominant intends to scene with his submissive.*

Slave   a BDSM role. A slave assigns ownership or rights over themselves to their partner.

Squick   to cause to feel repulsion, to disgust.

Submissive  a BDSM role. A submissive hands over control over some of their activities to their partner for the length of a scene or longer term if they live together.

Switch   a person who can adopt the role of top or bottom to suit their own and their partner's needs.

Suspension  a type of rope bondage where the person being tied is first tied and is then suspended in the air from a frame or from a bolt in the ceiling.

Top  a BDSM role. A top is the one who does things to their partner, the bottom, during a scene. This could be bondage, spanking, caning, flogging, and so on.

Toys  Equipment used for BDSM play such as floggers, canes, chains, cuffs, etc.; hence *toy bag*, i.e., a bag used for carrying around BDSM equipment.

# About the author

Peter Masters is a BDSM dominant and author who lives in Sydney, Australia. He has enjoyed taking control of fine women since his early twenties (which was thirty years ago) and is the author of a number of BDSM and kinky-sex-related books.

He has a website, which is more a wiki than anything else, where you can find hundreds of articles on BDSM and related topics:

```
http://www.peter-masters.com/
```